THE BIRTH OF THE CHRISTIAN FAITH

THE BIRTH
of the
CHRISTIAN FAITH

JAMES McLEMAN

OLIVER AND BOYD
EDINBURGH AND LONDON
1962

OLIVER AND BOYD LTD
Tweeddale Court
Edinburgh 1
39A Welbeck Street
London W 1

FIRST PUBLISHED 1962

PRINTED IN GREAT BRITAIN BY
OLIVER AND BOYD LTD., EDINBURGH

Contents

Introductory

CHRISTIANITY is believed to be a supernatural religion in the sense that it owes its origin to the divine intention and its ultimate explanation is in the mind of God. This cannot be proved and therefore every Christian is so by an act of faith.

Since, however, Christianity has a history as everything known to man must have, it is theoretically possible to explain its existence in terms of cause and effect, to trace it forward and backward from any given point in its existence in terms of its modifications, to point to an interval of time on one side of which it existed and on the other it did not.

Theoretically this must be so, without prejudice to its supernatural origin. Church historians act on this assumption. They are accustomed to investigate the ethos and conditions of an age, the actions and motives of men, for the very purpose of explaining why and how Christianity was of a particular nature at a particular time. If they confess that they are unable to give a satisfactory explanation at any point, it is not because they doubt the principle but because they lack the material or the ability to interpret it. Even so, they will continue to try to give a coherent account of their subject by the use of hypotheses.

Beginning from our own time, it is possible to conceive of giving a continuous account of Christianity back to the period when it can be said without fear of contradiction: "We have reached the time when Christianity has not yet begun to exist." But this account would become less and less complete in the process, in the sense that deduction would increase in relation to demonstration. In consequence, the history of Christianity in the first century of its existence is based on a limited quantity of materials which gives rise to a vast number of deductions or hypotheses, many of them irreconcilable. Pages could be filled of subjects arising out of the existence of Christianity in the first century on which there is no consensus of opinion, this in spite of the fact that all concerned in the study are dependent on the same data.

This, of course, does not mean that the whole of Christianity in the first century is equally hazy. It means that on some points we are relatively well informed while on others we are ignorant. We are like an excavator who finds one or two stones *in situ* and is anxious to know what kind of building stood there. But when he makes his reconstruction, other experts may disagree on some points. They do not doubt that a building existed on this site, nor do they doubt that it is theoretically possible to reconstruct it. But (to continue the metaphor) what did it really look like? If we want to know we must qualify ourselves to discriminate between the possibilities. Otherwise we must be content with the simple general fact that a building of some kind stood on this spot; for which indeed there is sufficient evidence.

As far as the beginnings of Christianity are concerned, the average Christian is satisfied that the foundations exist in the first century. He looks at the Gospels, Acts, and Epistles and is content as indeed he may be. But if we wish to reconstruct the beginnings we must start the arduous and precarious process of imaginative re-creation.

There is no escaping this. Anyone who thinks the first years of Christianity are there in the New Testament and all that requires to be done is to fit existing parts together, might as well try to make a complete building out of a few stones. What we have to do is to deduce the building from the size, shape and position of the few stones, which is something quite different, more feasible and very exciting.

This is what New Testament scholarship has been engaged in for the past century. Many experts have been on the field and there is a large area of agreement. But it must be acknowledged that a vast amount of work has yet to be done and little hope that the possible will ever become the actual—a complete account of the rise of Christianity.

It is therefore best to face at the outset the fact that the materials available for a history of the beginnings of Christianity are very meagre. The earliest Christian document extant (Galatians or, as some think, I Thessalonians) was written about the middle of the century when Christianity had already been in existence for twenty years or more.

If we enlarge our view in a search for more data we must allow for the fact that this takes us still further from the actual events. If we take in the next fifty years to A.D. 100 we are still far from having a complete New Testament. The consensus of scholarly opinion would forbid us to count on the Johannine Gospel and Epistles, II Peter, Jude, and the Pastorals, and would warn us that most of what remains belongs to the last quarter of the century. Apart from canonical writings, all that our review would add would be the Christian epistle known as II Clement and less than half a dozen very cursory references in pagan writers.

Thus the literary materials are scarce. And further, they are not designed to tell us what we want to know since their interest is not ours. Not one of the documents can be exactly dated, many cannot be assigned to a definite author, all may have been edited by later hands. These facts are the measure of the bewildering task confronting students of the earliest period. They explain why every document and doctrine is still matter of debate. They also help to explain why Church historians include both inflexible traditionalists and irrepressible nonconformists.

But the prospects are not quite so bleak as might appear. Books are made out of the experience of the past. They incorporate earlier traditions that may or may not be sound. They reveal conditions that presuppose earlier conditions. In a manner of speaking every document is a torch which sheds some of its light backwards.

The New Testament scholar gropes back into the silent days of Christianity with the help of these torches. He tries to see and note all the evidence there is and then tentatively to reconstruct the period. He is, of course, a fool if he imagines there can be anything sacrosanct about his reconstruction.

It may be objected that the Book of Acts is the authoritative story of the first years from the beginning of the Church to the Roman imprisonment of Paul. Why not accept it and be grateful?

We cannot bypass historical criticism in this fashion. It is not simply that Acts is a small book and omits many things most interesting to us. No scholar is prepared to say with certainty who wrote it, when and why. It is a composite work and the only apparently contemporaneous material is the "We" passages. The compiler is himself trying to reconstruct a period beyond his own personal knowledge, perhaps from very inadequate sources of varied quality. His reconstruction is not in the interest of what we call history but under the constraint of prescribed necessities which render him unable or unwilling to exercise historical discrimination such as is required today.

This is far from saying that Acts is not a conscientious work of unique value. On the contrary, it is the work of a man of strict standards of accuracy. But simply for that reason and because his purpose is not ours the Book of Acts cannot fulfil our need. We might have been better served by a collector rather than a compiler.

The historian cannot be but glad to have this material,

but on condition that he is free to use it as he would use other available data. He will acknowledge that he has the responsibility of discriminating in cases where, for example, Acts and Galatians disagree; and he will feel no obligation to uphold Acts simply because it seems to be in the form of a history whereas Galatians is an epistle.

These facts so far stated are neither new nor startling. They reveal a situation in the first century *vis-à-vis* Christianity which is in no respect surprising. There was no reason why pagan authors should give us useful information about Christianity in its obscure beginnings. There is every reason to be grateful that so much has in fact survived from the first century.

The reason for covering this ground is to pin-point the truth that anyone wishing to get into the skin of the first years of Christianity must be prepared to be venturesome and risk making big mistakes. If he plays safe all the time he will never touch the pulse of that new life.

Too many histories of the early Church are not the history of a movement at all but a stereotype. It as is if, instead of a portrait, we were presented with a drawing of an ancient suit of armour which never lived and never could have lived. Dogma has written most of our Church history; too often truth and life have been sacrificed in the interest of preconceived pattern. What doesn't fit is ignored or trimmed to shape; this nearly always seems preferable to adopting a fresh hypothesis.

What follows is an investigation into the brief period immediately following the Crucifixion. Some will think it rash or worse; no one will regard it as authoritative. One thing is certain. It does nothing to weaken any conviction about the uniqueness of Jesus or to undermine faith in the supernatural inception of the Christian movement in history.

The Crucial Interval

IT may be said that the birth of Christianity is hidden in the tomb of Jesus. When the tomb was no longer significant to Jesus' disciples, Christianity was already born; but so long as their hearts were with Jesus in death, they could not be aware of His presence in life. They were therefore unable to say the things which were later to make disciples in addition to their own number. The birth of Christianity took place when some person or some company of persons turned away (metaphorically) from the tomb, saying, "He is not here: He is risen."

It is true that the tomb once again became significant, but in a quite different way—when "He is risen" became "He was raised." That this is not simply a quibble about a form of words can be seen if we reflect on certain facts which belong to the nature of temporal awareness. The experience of the first person to realise that Jesus is not dead is not the same thing as the belief by subsequent persons that He was raised from the dead. The initial experience is creative; the later experiences may be only confirmatory or imitative. Further, to the subsequent experiencer the initial experience has become history.

This is not to deny that all who believe that Jesus is alive share something in common which entitles them all to be called Christians. But there is a unique quality belonging to the first affirmation of such a faith as far as Christianity regarded as a movement is concerned. It may mean that the first affirmation becomes history in a sense which all following affirmations can never bear.

The subsequent story confirms this in various ways. There is evidence that those who were of the original group

6

when the first affirmation was made had a unique place in the Church, principally Peter. Even in the second century, a teacher who had had contact with one believed to have been of that select company was specially revered. When the Church was fighting heresy it relied upon the words and deeds of those who were there when everything began.

Again, the second generation of believers (even the first generation, apart from those later called Apostles), experience the benefits of Christian fellowship, but depend on the word of the Apostles for the assurance that Christ is risen. There is no evidence that every new believer had his own specially repeated revelation of the Risen Christ, although he did enjoy the blessings that flowed from believing in the Risen Christ. In the first instance he believed the word, the report, the witness of the Apostles (or of others concerning them) that Jesus is risen. His life was a Christian experience in the present. His faith, i.e. what he believed, was a received tradition. He believed on authority and that belief was essential to the Christian experience.

There is no ground for suggesting that early Christians each enjoyed their own personal experience which convinced them that Jesus is alive. The evidence is that they believed and found thereby the Christian experience. In theological terms, as the New Testament insists, faith precedes salvation.

The message to outsiders was to the effect that Jesus is alive on the testimony of a few and that He is concerned in a specific way with the destiny of every soul. Where possible, this message is reinforced from the Old Testament scriptures. It is not therefore a direct revelation to everyone who is to become a Christian, but in the first instance a proposition to be supported by witnesses and testimony. The experience of being a Christian is direct, but the creed

B

of the Christian is communicated. It is therefore historical and capable of being traced to its first moments.

But this particular analytical interest in its beginnings is not to be expected initially. It appears only after the apostolic age has almost gone. Even then it is not the kind of interest that we now take; and it has been satisfied by concrete stories in which the principal characters take part and the empty tomb is regarded as a further proof that Jesus was raised from the dead, in addition to the witness of the Apostles and the testimony of Old Testament scripture.

This interest in the tomb after Christianity has been in existence for some time, is quite different from the interest of the first disciples on the morrow of the Crucifixion. Once the certainty arises that He is risen, the tomb is of no consequence to the disciples except as a symbol of death having been destroyed. There is no reason to suppose that any early Christian ever made a pilgrimage to the tomb of Christ.

The reason why we must begin at the tomb, is simply because this is the latest point at which we are safe to say, "Up to now, Christianity does not exist." We shall need to go back beyond this in our investigation. But this is the *terminus a quo* for the crucial interval in which it can be said that Christianity was born. The *terminus ad quem* is not so readily fixed.

The question therefore confronts us: What is the interval between the burial of Jesus and the objective certainty that the Church is in existence? We are not yet concerned to ask what was the course of events between, for example, the Crucifixion and the Day of Pentecost. We simply ask: How long was it before the assurance which created the Church came into being? It might seem that this is a very limited and trivial subject of investigation and, in any case, it may be thought quite impossible to reach a conclusion. But it can be pointed out that unless we know the interval we cannot begin to study what happened in it and, secondly, that the paucity or doubtful validity of the materials at hand for answering such a question is no greater an obstacle than it is in some other inquiries. Scholars still debate about the day on which Jesus was crucified and the precise course of events on that day. The fact is, the immediate post-Crucifixion days are an epoch-making period of time whose duration is of great consequence. Nothing prevents us from examining what evidence there is and using the same kind of historical method here as elsewhere. Our interest requires us to do so.

Our first duty, then, is to survey all the material on the subject, irrespective of its provenance, and discover whether there is any unanimity on the question. If not, we must enquire whether there is any explanation of the disparity which would lead to probability. This is conventional practice.

Since we are concerned at present only with the evidence of the time lapse between the Crucifixion and the first sign of the distinctive Christian belief, it will be sufficient to summarise the data simply in the order in which the books appear in the New Testament.

MATTHEW:

Mary Magdalene and the other Mary go to the sepulchre towards dawn on the first day of the week. An angel shows the empty tomb, proclaims Jesus risen, and instructs them to tell His disciples He will meet them in Galilee. The women meet Jesus Himself on the way back. He greets them and they hold His feet and worship Him. He repeats the instructions just given. (XXVIII.1-10) In Galilee the eleven disciples meet Jesus as prearranged. They worship Him "but some doubted." He commissions them and promises His constant presence.

(XXVIII.16-20).

MARK:

> Mary Magdalene, Mary the mother of Jesus, and Salome go the tomb early on the first day of the week. The stone has been moved. An angel tells them Jesus is risen and instructs them to tell His disciples "and Peter" He will meet them in Galilee. The women depart hastily and say nothing of what had taken place.   (XVI.1-8)

LUKE:

> Women go to the tomb early on the first day of the week. The stone has been moved. Two angels remind them Jesus said He would be crucified and rise the third day. They return and tell the disciples. Some do not believe.
>   (XXIII.55-XXIV.12)
> The same day "two of them" go to Emmaus. A stranger joins them and instructs them on the scriptural necessity of Christ's death and resurrection. Only later do they realise the stranger was Jesus. They hurry back to Jerusalem with the news. In the meantime the disciples have heard that Jesus has appeared to Peter.
>   (XXIV.13-35)
> There and then He appears to them all, convincing them by showing His hands and feet and eating in their presence. He instructs them on the scriptural necessity of His death and resurrection and commissions them. He orders them to stay in Jerusalem till they are clothed with power. He leads them to Bethany, blesses them and departs.
>   (XXIV.36-52)

JOHN:

> Mary goes to the tomb early on the first day of the week. The stone has been moved. She goes and tells Peter and the "other" disciple. They run to the tomb. Peter enters followed by the "other" (who believes) and finds the tomb empty. They return to their homes. (XX.1-10)
> Mary weeps outside the tomb, speaks to the gardener

who is revealed as Jesus. He warns her not to touch
Him, tells of his imminent ascension and instructs her to
inform "my brethren," which she does.   (xx.11-18)
The same evening Jesus comes through closed doors to
His disciples, blesses them, shows His hands and side.
They rejoice, receive another blessing and are commissioned. He breathes on them, they receive the Holy
Spirit and the power to forgive and retain sins. The
appearance is repeated for Thomas's benefit and Jesus
blesses those who believe without seeing. We are told
that this is only a selection of His appearances.

(xx.19-30)

An appearance by the Sea of Tiberias. Peter and six
others are hailed from the shore by Jesus who tells them
to cast the net on the right side. The "other" disciple
recognises Jesus first. Peter then wades ashore, the others
draw net and boat to shore. A meal is prepared and
they have food from Jesus' hands. This, we are told, is
the third appearance.   (xxi.1-14)
An appearance by the sea for Peter's special benefit
("Lovest thou Me?"), ending with instructions to Peter
and a prophecy about his future. He is advised not to
be curious about the "other" disciple's future.

(xxi.15-23)

Acts:

Over a period of forty days Jesus gives proofs that He is
alive. He tells His disciples to wait in Jerusalem for
baptism by the Holy Spirit. They ask if He will now
restore the kingdom to Israel, and are told this is the
Father's secret. They will be His witnesses to the ends
of the earth. Jesus blesses them and disappears heaven-
wards. Two angels tell the disciples He will return in
the same way. The disciples (men and women) devote
themselves to prayer. Peter persuades them to appoint
someone in Judas' place. On the Day of Pentecost the

Spirit descends and Peter preaches to the multitude that Jesus is Messiah.   (I.1–II.36)

1 CORINTHIANS:

Christ rose again on the third day, according to the scriptures. He was seen by Peter, then by the twelve. After that He was seen by more than 500 brethren at one time. After that He was seen by James and then by all the apostles. Last of all by me (Paul).   (xv.4–8)

It is evident there is no unanimity, and the disparities in some cases are very glaring. Our sole concern at the moment is with time element. How long was it after the Crucifixion before there was certainty that Jesus is risen? We cannot safely come further from the Crucifixion than "the third day." Up to then there is no belief in the Risen Christ. That fixes the boundary for the crucial interval on the side nearest the Crucifixion. Is there any indication that it may be impossible to be as definite on the other side? And, if this is so, will this indicate that the conviction that Jesus is risen was arrived at by a gradual process? It is with these questions in mind at present that we consider the material at our disposal.

The indications of time in the New Testament records do not permit us to conclude immediately that one interval and only one can be fixed. There are four periods to consider in view of the emphasis placed on them in the different sources. No doubt their importance in the minds of those who handed down the traditions is variously interpreted and their records are not designed to answer our special question. At this stage we simply note them as significant periods in the transition we are investigating.

Firstly, there is the period spoken of as "the third day." The calculation includes the day on which Jesus was crucified. We should say within two days of the Crucifixion. It is further defined as the first day of the week.

Secondly, there is the interval which includes the disciples' journey from Jerusalem to Galilee. We have no way of being certain about the extent of this period. The disciples could have left Jerusalem immediately after Jesus was arrested, after the Crucifixion, or after the third day.

Thirdly, there is a "forty-day" interval which is considered by one source to be of very exceptional importance.

Fourthly, there is a period which extends as far into the early days of the Church as the conversion of Saul. This may be as much as two years but cannot be fixed.

It will be noted that so far we have not tried to evaluate sources. We have been content simply to take all the available material and ask what answer it gives to a specific question, namely, whether there are any indications of time contained in them.

The answer, we have discovered, is four. These are (a) "the third day," (b) a time allowing for a journey from Jerusalem to Galilee, (c) the end of a forty-days' interval, and (d) an indefinite period whose terminus is the conversion of Saul of Tarsus.

The importance attached to these times by any of the sources is left till later but we note these possibilities: that these times may be different answers to one question, that they may be four answers to four different questions, that they may be radically inconsistent, that they may be inconsistent due to misinterpretation of information on the part of one or other of the traditions.

One further point is to be made. It is that these times certainly take us beyond the birth moment of Christianity in the case of (d). They may do so at (c) or even at (b). They certainly do not at (a), in the sense that prior to "the third day" there was certainly no Christianity in existence.

The general and initial impression given is that the birth

moment of Christianity is indefinite in terms of time but the same persons appear in the various accounts. This may point to an element of gradualness in what we are investigating and directs our attention to the possibility of persons being more significant than times and places.

Analysis of the Material

IT is necessary that we should now take a closer look at the material on which any reconstruction of the critical period must be based. At this point we must begin to take note of the date and try to evaluate the quality of the material, in spite of the difficulties accompanying such a proceeding.

At the outset it must be stated that none of the documents can be exactly dated, but there is sufficient agreement among scholars to allow us to arrange them in their probable order. This order has reference to what we shall call date of publication, except in the case of the Pauline extract. We acknowledge also that the Gospels and Acts are composite works incorporating older sources, in some cases written, in others belonging to oral tradition. So it can happen that a late document may contain an early and valid tradition, perhaps in a modified form.

Our method must therefore be designed to guard against leaving us at the mercy of a matter of precise dating. So far, we have been able to avoid this possibility, but must now take the risk of being within reach of it without falling into its power.

The material is in four sections—the Pauline, the Synoptic, Acts, and the Johannine. It would be generally agreed that this is the order in time. It is sufficient to place 1 Corinthians within the first two or three years of the fifth decade, Mark, Matthew, and Luke within the period 70 to 85, Acts between 80 and 100, and the Johannine Gospel in the first decade of the second century. These approximate dates may not be universally agreed but the matter is not of great consequence for our purpose so long as the order is sound and the composite nature of the documents agreed.

1 CORINTHIANS:

This is certainly the earliest material we have. It is still nearly a quarter of a century after the crucial period and we have to admit possibilities of misunderstanding on the part of the author and take into account the setting of the extract.

Nevertheless, the fact that it is the earliest and that it is on the precise subject advises us to treat it with great respect. As far as the date of the events recorded is concerned, it is imprecise. The appearance to Peter and the others may have been on "the third day" or many days after. If, in one case, twelve were involved, does this imply an appearance after Judas' successor was appointed, or is it a slip, or were the twelve not yet known as apostles?

We note the only mention of James in relation to the first days. Also the identification of Paul's own experience with that of the others. The appearance to five hundred must be subsequent to the Ascension if we accept Acts 1.15, where it is said, "the number of names together were about an hundred and twenty."

It is quite clear that Paul has no first-hand knowledge of this matter and is re-telling what has been reported to him. He expects his readers to believe, in reference to the first days, on the evidence on which he himself has believed. We can take it that if he had had more or more convincing evidence he would have cited it.

MARK:

It is profitless to speculate on what a lost ending of Mark would be likely to contain. We note the introduction of (three) women into the narrative and the interest in the tomb and the stone. The "and Peter" may be significant and also the intimation that the scene is to be transferred to Galilee. There is no appearance of Jesus in this account.

MATTHEW:

Here (two) women go to the tomb and the narrative agrees with Mark but adds that the women did see Jesus on their return journey. The repetition of the instructions at so short an interval and in such circumstances might be an indication of later addition. The Galilee scene is realised as promised. The appearance did not convince some. It may be felt that with Matthew's account we have moved further away from the bare simplicity of 1 Cor. xv.

LUKE:

Contrast the length and detail here with the Pauline account. We take note of the education of the disciples regarding the meaning of Christ's death and resurrection— on three separate occasions. Women are there but there is no appearance to them and their story of the empty tomb is not generally believed.

The story of the Emmaus journey is unique. We note the inability to recognise Jesus and the report of the disciples that Peter (alone) has seen the Lord, in the first instance. In the final section are three additions—proof that the appearance is Jesus by sensible demonstration, the disciples forbidden to leave Jerusalem (no Galilee tradition), and the promise of power.

In Luke's narrative we feel perhaps for the first time that we are in the presence of a professional writer who has not simply told but self-consciously re-told the classic story.

JOHN:

Much new material appears here also. Only one woman

goes to the tomb. She does not at first recognise Jesus. Jesus speaks of His ascension. There are further sensible demonstrations. The Holy Spirit is conferred there and then along with power to forgive or retain sins. Two appearances are located in the north. There is a persistent attempt to thrust the "other" disciple into a place of prominence. This involves competition with Peter. It is evident that Peter's position in the crucial period is firmly established.

John's account appears to be bristling with theological and ecclesiological preoccupations. The impression is that the material is being moulded to serve other than historical or testimonial interests.

ACTS:

The account here is, of course, closely related to that in Luke and in these post-Crucifixion passages a similarity of style and interests is patent. Here we come upon the only mention of the forty-day period. The liaison between the end of Luke and the beginning of Acts is difficult, probably due to the introduction of the forty-day period and the necessity to record a bodily ascension. Teaching is given here also but concerning the kingdom. Peter is quite evidently the most prominent personality. The account reveals other characteristics valuable to a study of Luke-Acts but not pertinent to our immediate enquiry.

This short summary of the material shows that it grows with time, that in some respects it is far from self-consistent, that it varies according to its provenance. Bearing in mind that the earliest is a generation later than the event, though, like the others, having its roots in earlier times, it would be most rash to prefer any account out and out as against the other. A fair treatment of the material requires a much more difficult approach.

What is suggested now, therefore, is that we should

make a list of the features which this survey has thrust upon our attention with a view to finding out whether a closer investigation of any or all of them can bring us any nearer a more definite picture of the first creative days.

These are:

1. "The Third Day"
2. The Tomb and the Women.
3. Jerusalem and/or Galilee.
4. The Element of Unbelief.
5. Education on the Cross and Resurrection.
6. The Prominence of Peter.

We may treat (1) and (2) very briefly in this chapter, but the others will require much more detailed attention. They will involve us in an attempt to get inside the minds of the disciples during the significant period. This in turn will require some treatment of the expectations of the disciples prior to the Crucifixion. Meantime we turn to "The Third Day" and "The Tomb and The Women."

THE THIRD DAY

There is every reason to believe that "the third day" was conventional from an early date. It is so in the epistles of Paul, and this is confirmed by the formula, "according to the scriptures." It is not difficult to see how this would happen.

No one, apparently, could testify to seeing Jesus actually rising from the dead. This would have been the ultimate in testimony and, had it been available, it would certainly have been quoted from the very beginning. The next immediate possibility was to be aware that Jesus had just risen. The closer such witness approached the actual dividing line between death and life, the more striking it would appear and therefore the more effective as testimony.

It is evident, therefore, that the tradition regarding the Resurrection could be pressed no further than the earliest moment after the actual event. And, in the nature of the case, it was inevitable that this should in fact happen. The tradition could not come to a state of rest until that point had been reached. It is the only position for a *terminus a quo* for a completed corpus of Resurrection narrative.

"The third day" is not stated by Paul to be the date of the first appearance. We have seen that this question of time and place is not one which requires precision as far as he is concerned. It is sufficient for him that others are reported to have seen the Lord—as he himself has. That their experience preceded his own is neither here nor there and in no way distinguishes them from him. He has seen Christ as well as they.

In Mark "the third day" is still not the date of the first appearance: it is the date of preparation for appearance. But this is to take place only after the disciples have made the seventy-mile journey from Jerusalem to Galilee. It might be inferred that the appearances of Jesus belong not to the story of Jesus but to the story of the Church.

The other traditions are in complete agreement in setting down a confident and detailed account of events on "the third day," even to the point of stating in some cases the particular hour of the day. The accounts are not consistent but they are precise beyond anything in Paul and Mark. And they record appearances up to the earliest moment possible. This reveals progression in the tradition in accordance with the dogmatic expectation described above. It is evident therefore that the Resurrection tradition could have developed up to a precise position in the matter of time and that it did this very thing. In retrospect this position was bound to become the initial moment of the complete tradition regarding the whole event, the birth-hour of belief in the Risen Lord.

Once the necessity for a starting point is evident, it is readily fixed by predetermining and dogmatic necessities. It was not possible to go back beyond the supposed dividing line between life and death. An hour after the expiry, for instance, would certainly render the probability of a genuine death and resurrection suspect. If there is evidence of a belief that a certain period elapsed before the soul finally departed from the lifeless body, then that would determine the utmost reach of any Resurrection narrative— the third day. Such evidence may be present in John XI.39.

Other influences would confirm this; for instance, scriptural analogy. A passage such as Hosea VI.2 must have been full of significance to a generation which gathered testimonies as proofs of Jesus' Messiahship from the Old Testament scriptures in the fashion illustrated in Matthew's Gospel, for instance. In the reference to Jonah's being three days in the belly of the whale (Mt. XII.39) we have a very precise and ingenious instance. This passage (Mt. XII.38-42) is usually assigned to Q and paralleled in Lk. XI. 29-32. But Luke includes no reference to "three days." Jonah's mission is to warn of coming judgment, not to typify the Resurrection. At some stage, presumably later than Q, this Resurrection reference entered the tradition. But "the third day" was already conventional.

THE TOMB AND THE WOMEN

We have already seen that the tomb plays no part in the early belief in the Resurrection. The further we go from the date of the event, the more focal does the tomb become. This is to be expected. Tradition sharpens the total picture till both time and place have become precisely fixed and what is initially insignificant is burdened with a weight it was never expected to bear. The vague "somewhere" and "somewhen" is now "there" and "then."

This, it should be remarked, is not a surmise but a deduction from the material. The place is predetermined in precisely the same fashion as the time and, of course, must be co-ordinated with it. Documents are vague or silent as to both or clear and definite as to both. Paul has no mention of the tomb and the "third day", as we have seen, is conventional; Peter's reported speech mentions neither. On the other hand the Gospels give increasingly factual and pointed prominence to both.

We know nothing of how the bodies of those who incurred the full penalty of the criminal law were disposed of after their execution. Perhaps this has little bearing on what befell the body of one in particular. But if the earliest records tell us nothing on the subject, we must be cautious in accepting complete accounts coming from a much later period, especially if there existed a dogmatic gap requiring to be filled.

It follows that to try to answer such questions as "Who moved the stone?", is a speculation on a proposition which is itself speculative in the first place, and therefore a proceeding which can hardly be expected to establish any useful conclusion.

The presence of women in the later stories is not quite in the same category. That they should be represented as going to the tomb to embalm or to weep over the body of Jesus without making provision for admission to the tomb, is of a piece with the tomb tradition in the sense that it shows a growing point of the same organon.

However, the difficulty is in the fact that they are present at all. It seems impossible that they should be introduced into the story at a later stage in the tradition, and we must conclude that they were present in the initial moments of the belief.

The part they played shows development even within the Synoptic Gospels. In Mark there is no appearance to women. An angel informs them at the tomb of the great event. Matthew adds that on the way back Jesus Himself met and spoke with them. Luke enhances the story in the same direction. The Fourth Gospel adds its own even more precise details.

The association of women with the story, therefore, is that they went to find the body of Jesus and did not succeed. When and where, it may not be possible to determine in view of the necessities which pressed ever more heavily upon the two factors of time and place in the developing tradition. We are therefore, it would seem, bound to admit the presence of women at the beginning, but that they went to a tomb and that on the third day would require earlier and better testimony.

Location of the Appearances

WHEN we come to consider where the reported appearance of Christ after His Resurrection took place, we reach a point at which the traditional theologian most violently rebels against the historical approach to this subject. It is safe to say that, if all the records were in perfect agreement as to the location of these appearances, the witness of the historian would be welcomed. The fact is that no one can make all our authorities tell the same or even a consistent story. The gap between them is not simply a question of disparities but of contradictions.

Let us consider what this problem permits and does not permit us to do. If it is to be maintained that after His death Jesus made Himself known by appearing in some form to His disciples, and that this was not a matter of psychological awareness on the part of the disciples but of substantive proof conveyed by Jesus, then this is history in the same sense as the Crucifixion is history, and subject therefore to the same kind of historical investigation.

It follows from this that both theologians and historians are bound by certain conditions. If the theologian is anxious to maintain the historicity of the Resurrection, he must not try to rail off the post-Crucifixion period from historical investigation. He must not allow, for instance, freedom to decide whether the cleansing of the Temple took place at the beginning or the end of Jesus' ministry as a historical issue, but at the same time refuse to allow any decision on historical grounds as to where and when Jesus appeared after His Crucifixion.

Conversely, if the theologian is anxious to withdraw

the Resurrection from the province of the historian (e.g. for dogmatic reasons or in view of the contradictions), he must rest his case for belief in the Risen Jesus on a base not subject to historical scrutiny. If he says, "I believe because Peter or some other has reported," he must be content to allow the query whether it is true that Peter or some other has in fact done so. This is a historical inquiry. If he says, "I believe because I experience," this is a matter of religious psychology. But he cannot use his faith in the Resurrection as both a religious experience and an acceptance of an historical fact to forbid the investigation of the data from a historical point of view.

The historian is similarly situated. As historian he is not in a position to start the history of the Church from an assumption of miracle, unless he can prove that it has no explanation in terms of other historical events. It will not do to tell the story of Jesus up to the Crucifixion, interpolate a paragraph intimating a supra-historical event which cannot be described, and begin the Church's history from, for example, the Day of Pentecost, if, on the plane of history, he believes there is continuity between the life of Jesus and the beginnings of Church history. History has no gaps. It cannot be written on the assumption of discontinuity.

It is regrettable that many theologians and Church historians have never frankly recognised these conditions imposed by their disciplines. In view of the nature of the data of this period, they have both been anxious to secure the best of both worlds. The theologian wants a historical basis for his doctrine without the necessity to submit to the conditions of historical investigation. The Church historian has often been content to begin Church history as if a dogmatic basis were the equivalent in Church history of a historical basis in any other historical investigation. But, if we go in terror lest history disprove faith, then we are of all men most miserable.

We have seen that our earliest sources (the speeches of Peter in Acts and St. Paul's record in 1 Cor. xv) tell us nothing regarding time and place in relation to the post-Crucifixion appearances. As to our other authorities, Mark records no appearance but forecasts a meeting of Jesus and His disciples in Galilee. Matthew inserts an appearance to women in Jerusalem and relates an appearance in Galilee; Luke-Acts recounts appearances in the Jerusalem area and records an expressed command to the disciples not to leave Jerusalem; John records appearances both in Jerusalem and in Galilee.

The most obtrusive fact here is the isolation in which Luke-Acts stands as strictly confining all activities to the Jerusalem area. This is done not by default (as might be argued in the case of Mark's omission of all reference to Jerusalem appearances) but deliberately, and in such a way as to put the matter beyond all doubt.

The questions raised by this fact are much wider than our own concern. They must be taken into account in any estimate of the authorship and provenance of Luke-Acts. In their simplest form they are: Why does Luke-Acts confine appearances to Jerusalem? Was this a deliberate attempt to displace any tradition relating them to the north? How does it reflect on the historical reliability of Luke-Acts? Does it indicate a fluid state of post-Crucifixion tradition of such a nature as to discredit all attempts to locate appearances?

We are brought to such a pass in this investigation that it is difficult to decide how to proceed. Evidently no one can rest content with a vague notion that something happened but we know not what. Again, it is not possible to create a picture of this period in which every recorded incident will somehow find a place. Historically this is a position in which the records themselves compel us to discriminate against some or perhaps all of them.

Clearly it will not do simply to set aside Luke-Acts and try to harmonise the others into a consistent record. That, for one thing, is to treat part of a tradition as if it were the whole just for the sake of consistency. It is too easy—but, more important, it would not be honest—to work out the sum without taking the surd into account. This is evidently a proposition in which arbitrary selection of some data, even if it were legitimate, would not produce a reasonable conclusion. The indications are that a fundamental hypothesis of the documents themselves is at fault.

Luke-Acts succeeds in providing a consecutive story by confining the disciples in Jerusalem from the time of the Crucifixion to the Day of Pentecost. But in order to do so he has to depart from the other tradition or traditions in a radical fashion. Even so, the junction between Luke and Acts is not perfect. There is no suggestion in the last verses of Luke that the Ascension took place only after a period of forty days during which appearances of an unmistakable nature took place.

If we isolate what is peculiar to Luke-Acts, we have to include the following: the Emmaus incident, repeated instruction on the necessity for the death and Resurrection and its Old Testament authority, the command to wait in Jerusalem for power, repeated proofs over a period of forty days, the actual Ascension, the Day of Pentecost. This is surely a very formidable tradition and it makes all the more drastic the necessity to consider discarding it.

We should note here that, if we substract the last chapter of the Fourth Gospel as redactional, we are left with the fact that this Gospel originally had no account of appearances in the north. Luke-Acts therefore is not in the position of being an individualist reconstruction of events. It is representative of a stream of tradition which admitted no reference to Galilean appearances. The fact that the final chapter was added in the later edition of the Fourth Gospel, means that accommodation had to be made between two traditions at least. This again means that the state of post-Crucifixion tradition in at least one Christian centre was still fluid into the beginning of the second century.

If, however, we refuse to discard the "Jerusalem only" tradition, our other sources, which all contain references to appearances in Galilee, must be allowed to fall. This alternative is equally drastic, especially when we recall Luke's dependence on Mark for the basic outline of the life and last days of Jesus. We are thus in a cleft stick.

What we are investigating at present is the location of the assurance which created the Church in the first place. We are at a stand. Let us, then, remind ourselves that this is only part of our total subject which must embrace these three questions: Where did this occur? What was its nature? Who were its instruments? Our sources do not give a direct and unambiguous answer to the first question. If we press the question we find ourselves being forced to choose between two incompatible traditions. But we cannot feel justified in making such a choice.

It would seem, therefore, that we must either approach the question *de novo* on the basis of probability, or come to the conclusion that there is something which is inherently self-contradictory in the accounts themselves, or both. We cannot be satisfied to leave a historical investigation in a condition of such patent incongruity, especially when the incongruity arises out of our original data. Contradictions may equally be reactions to the same basic event. Only when we have discovered what the basic event is, are we aware of their relation and explanation.

The post-Crucifixion accounts cannot be understood except in the light of answers to the three questions above (What happened? Where? And to whom?), for they are effects deriving from the event itself. Conversely, from our side, the event itself is only arrived at through the account. This means that whatever solution we arrive at of the total problem must reveal both event and consequents as coherent circumstances in which contradictions find a necessary explanation.

We proceed first of all on the more limited investigation, namely that regarding the location of appearances, on the basis of probability. Is it possible to say where the initial events constituting the Church as a new movement in history took place?

The choice between Galilee and Jerusalem is formidable. Are we bound to make it, or is there some answer to the question, "What, in fact, happened?" which will admit of an answer requiring both locations?

There are events of this nature. The beginning of a new king's reign, for example, might conceivably lead to such a double emphasis. The question, "When was the king crowned?" can have only one precise answer, but "When did he become king?" might not. It might be answered by giving the moment when the old king died or by giving the date of the coronation. The question has, so to speak, both a private and a public answer. In some such way the answer to the question, "When was Christianity born?" might have a private and a public answer in which both Galilee and Jerusalem are involved as locations.

It is therefore not impossible that our variant traditions are due to a difference in emphasis which permits two answers to a question because the question is differently understood by the two traditions. The one answers Galilee and the other Jerusalem. It may be that they are dealing with a consecutive event. *In toto* it requires both locations, but what happened in each location is distinct from what happened in the other. If this composite and consecutive nature of the event is not realised, it is easy to conceive how the two component traditions will become rivals. Both will claim priority under the impression that they are speaking of the same event which they consider unitary.

Let us suppose that this total event, which is distinguished by two consecutive points of emphasis, is regarded as the fact that Jesus is risen or the fact that the Church is born. All accounts of Resurrection appearances in our material would then be regarded as answers to the question: When and where did it happen? The answers are two: Galilee, Jerusalem. We need not concern ourselves with the fact that one tradition is obviously aggressive in its anxiety to exclude the other. This is natural and readily explicable in the circumstances we postulate.

Now if one tradition arose through concentration on the primary fact that the first awareness of the total event must have been private, and the other through concentration on the fact that the reference of the total event is public, indeed universal, then we are able to see how both arose and how both grew in importance side by side. Both could be true but they are not referring to precisely the same circumstance, although to the same event.

Luke-Acts' emphasis on Jerusalem is completely understandable on this hypothesis. The author maintains that the Church was born, as an agent of the Gospel in the world, at Jerusalem on the Day of Pentecost. Significantly, it is he who refuses to countenance any reference to appearances in Galilee. His account of the appearances is entirely consistent with his thesis that Jerusalem is both the birthplace and the headquarters of the Church. If the Luke-Acts documents had not maintained the Jerusalem reference in regard to the appearances, our two-part event hypothesis would not have stood.

But the public manifestation of the event must be subsequent to the private aspect—indeed, consequent on it. The beginning of the Church as the agent of the Gospel in the world is possible only because the necessary dynamic for its creation is already a reality in someone's consciousness. And it is this facet of the event which is creative to the Galilee tradition. Priority in time belongs to Galilee. Priority in importance as far as Luke-Acts is concerned belongs to Jerusalem. These two priorities are not mutually exclusive. The total event embraces them both.

As regards the priority in time of the Galilee portion of the total event, there is every necessary support for it. It is practically impossible to reverse the order, unless we are prepared to renounce the whole framework of Luke-Acts. The Jerusalem tradition can be understood if it follows the Galilee tradition but not vice versa.

Without going into a detailed examination of the pre-Crucifixion story, it will be admitted that the disciples looked upon Jesus' journey to Jerusalem with foreboding, that Jesus never visualised the death of any of them along with Himself as a consequence, that the Last Supper was (whatever else) a farewell meal, that there was no expectation they should remain in Jerusalem after the arrest of Jesus (since they did not believe then in His Resurrection) and that the danger of their being taken into custody, contrary to the expressed wish of their Master, was considered to be very real. All these facts, each of which might well be amplified, make it highly probable that the disciples did not remain in Jerusalem from the arrest to the Day of Pentecost. They fled. Whither? There can be only one answer. It explains why in the first instance it was not possible to represent men as being among those who sought for the body of Jesus on the third day.

What happened in Galilee we are not yet in a position to discuss. But that the initial thing, without which there would be no Christian Church, took place in the north, there seems no reason to doubt. And that this was followed by a starkly public event in Jerusalem is the logical conclusion from our evidence.

Acts presents a picture of the disciples existing furtively in Jerusalem till the Day of Pentecost, whereupon with great boldness they publicly declare their faith that Jesus is risen. The contrast is deliberate. But, if our reconstruction is correct so far, the most amazing thing that took place was not a public demonstration in a state of exultation, but the seventy mile return journey of the disciples from Galilee to Jerusalem where, on their last unforgettable visit, Jesus had been crucified.

So often in tradition the nuance is right but the accent is in the wrong place. This can explain the double tradition regarding the appearances and also the contrast between a fearful little group in Jerusalem and a band of new-inspired men walking back to the city which had crucified their Lord.

The Element of Unbelief

BECAUSE we are now about to enter a different phase of our investigation, it will be convenient to review the phase through which we have passed. We began by delimiting the area with which we are concerned. It is the shortest interval between the time when it is possible to say, "No Christianity exists yet" and the time when it can be said, "Christianity is now in existence." What happened within that interval is our subject, in other words the birth of the Christian faith.

We found that the conventional limits of this interval are from the "third day" to the "Day of Pentecost." Within that period, our records inform us, relations between Jesus (who had been crucified) and his disciples were renewed. An analysis of the records revealed that there are not only disparities but contradictions. These presuppose a growth in tradition regarding what took place. This required that the "third day" must be the conventional beginning. The traditions themselves predispose us to consider the total event as one which is capable of a double, consecutive emphasis. This is the only premise which can account for the contradictions, in particular with regard to the location of appearances.

We have shown that there is reason to believe that after the Crucifixion the disciples returned to Galilee, and that it is there and then that we must find the initial indications of the event which we call the birth of the Christian faith.

In the course of our analysis of the material at our disposal, we found that we are trying to come to grips with one event which requires for its understanding the answers to three questions. These are:

1. Where and when did it occur?
2. What was its nature?
3. Who were its instruments?

So far we have dealt with the first of these only. We now proceed to consider the whole subject, not in terms of time and place, but primarily in terms of the nature of the occurrence to which the traditions bear witness.

It will be recalled that all the matters so far dealt with arise directly out of a close examination of the records. Among the points we noted as prominent features of the whole corpus of tradition, were the "third day," the women and the tomb, Jerusalem and/or Galilee. We have now reviewed these, and the next is the title of this chapter—the element of unbelief.

It will readily be seen that with this subject we are indeed entering on a new phase. It is new in two respects. Up to now we have been concentrating on time and place; now our attention is on event. Up to now our primary interest has been in the external scene; now we turn to the experience.

It is true that these are not separable: experience and event take place in time and space whatever else may be said about them. Our plea has been for the recognition of this fact as opposed to the tendency to introduce discontinuity into the experience and so make time and place irrelevant. We consider them separately because this is how they arise in the course of investigation, not because we imagine they are independent of each other. The stage is set before the play begins; no play can be played nowhere. Appearances and experiences must take place in the life of someone at some place, and to this general truth the records bear witness.

But having said this, we are not thereby obliged to conclude that the records of the event with which we have to do are *ipso facto* complete and beyond the reach of examination. Especially is this so since, as is the case, no *prima facie* consistency arises out of them. This is precisely the matter on which we are now engaged.

Our traditions present us with this unexpected and unexplained fact. The central constituent of the total event was not self-evidencing to all who were confronted with it. Some did not believe, did not know, did not recognise, required further proof. Why was this so? What light does it throw upon the nature of the occurrence? What new kind of demonstration was possible, or what could a time-interval effect in order that unbelief should become belief or failure to recognise become recognition?

These are very perplexing questions if we elect to take the accounts simply at their face value. We are in the presence of a direct encounter between persons well known to each other. It would seem impossible in the nature of the case that time or repetition could do what the initial person-to-person relationship had failed to do. Yet there is no question of disguise or deliberate attempt to confuse. On the contrary, the declared purpose of the appearances is to assure and convince, and the *raison-d'etre* of the record of the whole encounter is frustrated if this is not so.

This difficulty is sometimes explained away by postulating a state of mind (in those who were not convinced) which made the exercise of ordinary faculties of recognition unreliable. But such a presupposition raises more problems than it solves. Why, for instance, the discrimination as between persons passing through a common experience and confronted with the same phenomenon? Is it the distrait or the other who recognises, believes, requires no further proof? It would be difficult on this ground to withstand the argument that hallucination explains all.

Once again there is the temptation to give up the quest for a continuous account of the event to which our records unanimously if confusedly point back. It met us when we considered the discrepancies in the matter of time, and again in the matter of place. Now, when we ask, "What did occur?" we are confronted with the same inducement to retire and hand the whole matter over to the theologians, who will claim the event as historical but not subject to historical investigation.

If we refuse to deliver this foundational episode over to contingency, we must begin by realising clearly the situation in which we find ourselves. It is impossible to accept the records as they stand as a self-consistent account of the event. This has been freely recognised by scholars for many years. The element of unbelief is inexplicable if it refers to the recognition of a person who is presumed to be intent on establishing his identity in the presence of intimate friends.

This presumption, which is inalienable from the records, may appear to some to be questionable. But there is no way of establishing personal identity in a matter like this except through likeness at the very least. If certainty is required, and the sources insist on certainty (i.e. it was not someone like Jesus but Jesus Himself), then even likeness is not sufficient. Nothing less than identity in the sense of one-and-the-sameness will do. Jesus could not convince His disciples that He was Jesus by appearing to be quite unlike Jesus. Yet the records require that to some He should be certainly identical with Jesus, but to others at the same time He should not even resemble Himself.

Such contradictions cannot be resolved on the basic assumption—that He appeared in corporeal form to His disciples. Must we then abandon the assumption? This, it should be noted, would not require us to adopt a theory of hallucination. It need not commit us, and indeed must not, to any conclusion which is not sufficient to account not only for the existence of the traditions but for the growth of those traditions in particular.

Two facts must be reckoned with, facts which our earlier assumption of bodily appearances cannot cope with: (1) the possibility of opposite conclusions existing side by side in relation to the event, i.e. this is Jesus and this is not Jesus, and (2) the possibility that time can have any effect on the conclusions, i.e. that some did not believe initially but later were quite convinced, when in fact nothing different had happened external to themselves to account for the change.

These two facts are related primarily to the apprehension of the disciples. In no case in the tradition (except, perhaps, in the Fourth Gospel and in apparent recognition of this precise difficulty) is the bodily appearance represented as subject to unpredictable alteration in form. The emphasis of the tradition in this respect is upon the ability or otherwise of the disciples to recognise that the appearance is the appearance of Jesus. There seems to be nothing which the appearance could do to convince the unconvinced except simply to be itself, i.e. the appearance of Jesus. Belief and unbelief is not equated in the records with more likeness or less likeness to Jesus in appearance. It is the personal reaction of the disciple to the fact in whose presence he stands.

This means that the belief or unbelief is not represented as a matter of over-riding compulsion from without, but that it is a conclusion arrived at by normal human process as far as it applies to conviction and belief. It is belief not by fiat but by conclusion, by reaching that point along the normal psychological pathway that habitually leads to belief. The content of this belief is not yet our concern. We are merely establishing that the upshot of the event which is enshrined in the traditions was, in fact, a conviction arrived at in the same way as any human conviction is arrived at.

It is necessary to recapitulate the argument to this point. Among those present at the critical time and place were some who did not believe. This is so embarrassing to the later tradition that it must be regarded as of great authenticity. Since the purpose of the appearance as recorded is to convince, and any attempt to confuse is excluded, we must conclude that the passage from unbelief to belief, from failure to recognise to recognition, was due to modifications in the mind of those concerned and not to variation in the phenomenon itself. It is represented in this way in the record.

But if what we have called the phenomenon was a bodily appearance of Jesus, it is impossible, as has been shown, to account for the element of unbelief. We are therefore under the necessity to modify the assumption. But such modification must account for the traditions and for those features of the traditions which it is impossible to accommodate.

The suggestion is made, therefore, that all these factors are immediately seen to be congruous if the effective phenomenon at the very centre is not a bodily appearance which results in questions as to whether "it" is there or not or whether "it" is identifiable or not, but a new conception of who and what Jesus is.

We arrive at the conclusion, therefore, that what occurred at the critical time and place was not simply an appearance which is capable of being testified to by those who witness it, and denied by those who do not, but a revelation of truth which is capable of being simultaneously apprehended by some and not by others initially, but later is truly apprehended by all. If it is felt that something other than this must be postulated in addition, it should be noted that this "other" is not necessary to account for the records and indeed, of itself, is not capable of doing so. It should further be noted that the appearance interpreted as corporeal is not necessary to account for the belief, but, contrariwise, the belief may very well account for the records of bodily appearance.

This latter statement may appear to be the complete contrary of the general appraisal of the matter. But if the statement is considered, it is simply an assessment that just any man who rises from the dead is not the Christ of the Christian faith. The core of the whole event is the question, "Who and what is Jesus?" The answer to such a question cannot be found in a post-Crucifixion appearance in isolation. It is the conclusion of a process of intense preoccupation with the known facts of the life of Jesus. It is impossible to cut the birth of the faith off from the active ministry of Jesus and the association of disciples with Him in the period before His death. The Church was conceived during His ministry though it was not born till after His death.

What the content of the revelation or conviction was we must leave to the next chapter. But it is conceivable that it was such that it could not be expressed except in terms of a nature which accounts for the traditions. It is extremely difficult for us to appreciate the thought forms of Palestine in the first century. This is admitted in the interpretation of the sayings of Jesus. It would be agreed that Resurrection itself in the Hebrew connotation is a category alien to Graeco-Roman thought. Did it express in the pre-Christian tradition something which had no counterpart in the thought of any other people?

We read in the Old Testament of a prophet besieged by foreign troops. The heart of his servant sank. The prophet prayed, "Lord, I pray Thee, open his eyes that he may see." The narrative continues: "And the Lord opened the eyes of the young man; and he saw: and, behold, the

D

mountain was full of horses and chariots of fire round about Elisha" (II Kings VI.17). It may be asked whether we know what this means and if so whether we should express it in the same way.

The possibility is that no other way was open to express what happened at the birth of Christianity except the way that was taken. And this in itself would be a measure of the unprecedented nature of the occurrence. The expression of some experience hitherto beyond knowledge and belief, creates its own problem. How can one express what has never been expressed before? The choice is silence or the extravagant use of what has been already known or believed. The choice of silence was not open to the disciples.

Event or Conviction

WE have been forced to the conclusion that bodily appearances cannot account for the form and content of the traditions in the post-Crucifixion story. It has been argued that the phenomenon at the centre of the traditions is not an objective event but a conviction arrived at by normal process and that this explains the patent discrepancies of the traditions.

The Resurrection regarded as an objective event is thought to be so central to the Christian theology that this interpretation must be prepared to meet massive traditional and psychological opposition. We therefore pause here to consider whether it is possible to maintain our position.

To the theologian the Resurrection is autogenous and *a priori*. It is a new, miraculous, historically uncaused phenomenon which initiates consequences but can have no mundane antecedents. Christian doctrine has accordingly concentrated almost exclusively on what can be deduced from it and scarcely at all on the context in which it is found. The comparative neglect of the bearing of inter-Testamental Jewish theology on this matter by all but a few scholars proves this.

Can one maintain the historicity of an event which is conceived as having none of its causes in time and most of its consequences in supra-mundane terms? Could such an event be integrated into meaningful relation with the rest of life? Now we know of no effect in history which has God for its sole cause. And to postulate such an event would be to substitute supposition for necessary connexion in a case in which necessary connexion alone will be sufficient.

Before a dogmatic pronouncement which precludes investigation of possible causes is accepted, the history and context of an idea or event should be examined. If this door is closed to the historian, it is closed also to the theologian. The latter will no longer be able to claim an effective relationship between doctrine and meaningful existence. The theologian will have become a theosophist.

Consequently, if belief in the Resurrection is claimed to be more than a fascinating speculation, the historical approach is imperative. And once it is permitted it may or may not confirm the doctrine to which the theologian is committed. Certainly by its nature it cannot be bound to do so.

In the remainder of this chapter, therefore, I propose to do two things. The first is to examine briefly the history of the idea of resurrection in the pre-Christian period, the second is to remark on the alleged psychological necessity for some kind of objectivity in the experience of the disciples in the post-Crucifixion period, even when the belief in physical Resurrection has been surrendered. This is often urged as an argument for a position imagined to lie between the Scylla of hallucination and the Charybdis of resurrection of the flesh.

The idea of resurrection is strictly dependent on the idea of God; eschatology is an outgrowth from theology. To put it more concretely by example, you cannot believe in eternal punishment unless your God allows you to do so.

But theology does not immediately and automatically affect eschatology. There is a time-lag. Ultimately a genuine belief in God permeates all—worship, ethics eschatology. But it often happens that the full impact of a theology is only potential. Thus a professed belief in God may live side by side with an incomapatible ethic or eschatology which belongs with and arises from a more primitive conception of God.

The doctrine of God takes time to modify the various departments of our thought. It would seem to affect our ideas about the future life last of all.

Old Testament history had run most of its course before belief in resurrection was possible. Sheol dominated eschatology even when the eighth-century prophets had enlarged and ennobled the Hebrew conception of God. Men continued to feel bound to see God's justice and mercy worked out in their present life, for beyond was only the literally God-forsaken barrenness of the underworld.

The breakthrough came in two directions—in the direction of the thrust first of national hope and second of individual hope. The development of eschatological beliefs was a dynamic result of the frustrations of practical experience (both in national and in individual history) and the invincible hope in God which would not allow that frustration is the meaning of life.

The upshot is first, belief in a coming kingdom on the earth in which the nation will be justified before the world and enjoy abundant prosperity, and, secondly, belief in a blessed immortality for the individual man whose whole trust is in God. It is the meeting of these two that generates belief in resurrection. Individual saints are to be raised to enjoy the blessings of the kingdom on earth with those alive at the time. This is a bodily resurrection on this earth to an earthly kingdom which will last for ever.

But further experience continues to modify eschatology. It comes to be thought that this world can never be suitable for an eternal kingdom of God. This thought makes possible many variations on the theme of what must come to pass. The creation of a new heaven and a new earth, the limited duration of the earthly kingdom, the extended scope of the resurrection, these and many other new conceptions found a place in the eschatological programmes of the time.

It is recognised that out of the profusion of eschato-logical agitation between 200 B.C. and A.D. 100 many rival schedules of the course of future events were drawn up. The questions at issue were numerous. They were widely and vigorously debated. We should be mistaken in supposing that only professional theologians and book-producers discussed the nature of the Coming Kingdom, the re-surrection body and the God-appointed Man.

These are matters on which it is not possible or necessary to discover a consensus of opinion or to excogitate con-sistency. Hopes take small account of incompatabilities. It is only necessary to recognise that this is the fervent and turbid background against which the New Testament teaching on eschatology and resurrection must take its place.

Belief in the resurrection of Jesus in particular did not, perhaps could not, arise except where there already existed belief in resurrection in general. This is not to say that the one created the other, which is hardly possible. But the one is the context of the other and to that extent a cause.

In those eschatologies which foretold an eternal kingdom in a new heaven and new earth, it is the reclothed spirit that is the bearer of personality. The present body cannot enter this kingdom any more than the present earth can be its locus. It is the kingdom of glory and all who dwell in it are likewise glorified.

When we enquire concerning the eschatology of Jesus on the evidence of the Synoptic Gospels, it is apparent that it postulated a new heaven and new earth, preceded by a time of trouble culminating in universal judgment. The Law will abide till heaven and earth pass away. The right-eous shall shine as the sun (be glorious) in the kingdom of their Father. There are frequent references to a time of catastrophe. The theme of judgment in which the righteous are welcomed to everlasting glory and the wicked depart to everlasting doom is prominent.

Regarding the nature of resurrection in Gospel teaching, the evidence is that those who enter into eternal life do so in a transformed mode of existence. The present body is of so little account that it is not to be saved and its loss is not to be feared. The main aim is to live so faithfully that it is possible to enter into the life to come.

In argument with the Sadducees Jesus says the life to come is like that of the angels, a different order of being from man. This passage (Mk. xii.18-27 and parallels) is followed by an interesting exposition which implies that resurrection is not always essential. Abraham and the patriarchs are now alive in God's presence, i.e. before the resurrection period. Jesus argues not that the dead are raised but that (at least some of) the dead live. This is not exceptional since there is evidence of similar belief regarding Enoch, Moses, and Elijah.

The absence of consistency we have noted seems to have prevailed in the early Church. Resurrection was confidently expected as a prelude to the kingdom, but the temporary fate of the believer who died in the meantime could not be left in abeyance. The question was vigorously discussed in Corinth and it would be rash to assume that Paul's was the only or even a generally accepted answer. In Philippians 1.23 it is said that to depart this life is to be with Christ—even before the time at which the dead in Christ are to be raised. The dying thief could be with Christ on that very day without, apparently, a resurrection experience in the conventional sense.

What these considerations seem to make plain is that the teaching about resurrection in the first century was not a unity. It was a congeries of thought belonging to different stages of development in which primitive reposed side by side with the most advanced. Systematic eschatology was, perhaps must be, impossible.

As regards the teaching of Jesus, there are indications

that the centre of interest was not the mode of transition to eternal life but the urgency of attaining it. The word "resurrection" is not of frequent occurrence and is used probably always in answer to a question. (Curious questions are positively discouraged). While it is precarious to draw strict conclusions from this it can hardly be argued that this precise subject of resurrection was prominent in His teaching.

The life to be lived now, in order to attain the life to come which is a transformed existence, looms large. It is far from clear that this life to come depends on the act and fact of resurrection rather than on the established relationship with God, as in the prophets and psalmists.

If we suppose Jesus to have told His disciples He would rise on the third day (and this is fraught with grave objections), it is not proved that He encouraged them to expect resuscitation such as the later Gospel tradition insists on. The Church's subsequent canonisation of the doctrine of the resurrection of the flesh (modified to body), arose from dogmatic necessity—the need to combat gnosticism made it doubly necessary.

Now there are three general reflexions that arise from a study of this subject of resurrection. The first is that it was not and could not be deduced from experience; it was not an intellectual conclusion on the basis of evidence, but was born of the proleptic reach of faith. It was not so much something drawn out of experience as something thrown ahead so as to be joyfully encountered in experience yet to come. Briefly, the doctrine of resurrection is in the first instance the creation of the human spirit in its relation to God and the future.

Secondly, the thought was clothed in whatever garment was appropriate and available at the particular time. This depended on what would be allowed by the believer's doctrine of God, the world and man; and this was a matter

in which variation was possible and took place. Bodily
and spiritual resurrection lived side by side in the same
period. The range is from the Sadducees who renounced
all apocalyptic speculation, to those who tended to regard
the mode of resurrection as entirely secondary or even
substituted immortality for resurrection.

This brings us to the third fact, which is that the essence
and content of the doctrine is a union with God that nothing
can destroy. This is the primal faith which expressed itself
in relation to the future as the doctrine of resurrection. It
is not itself a hope but a present reality. It gives rise to a
hope and that hope expresses what the present reality will
ultimately be seen to be when it has inevitably won its
victory over every possible impediment.

It is therefore evident that resurrection is not so much
a proof of the inviolability of God's relation with the
believer, as an inference therefrom. From the manward
side it is not an event which leads to the conclusion that
there is life after death: it is itself a conclusion from the
present faith that nothing shall separate us from the love
of God.

This is the context of New Testament resurrection. It
is a fulfilment of prophecy and apocalyptic, in line with the
history of the idea and having the same content and the
same origin, the garment in which it is clothed, as ever,
being conditioned and secondary. Great spiritual con-
victions which are the fruit of ventures of faith are not
readily inherited. They tend to be absorbed by being
reduced to their most public and least strenuous
formula. The greatest are most likely to suffer from crass
materialisation.

The conclusion therefore that this phenomenon at the
centre of the post-Crucifixion experience of the disciples
is a conviction rather than an event, is continuous with
what we have found in our survey of the history of the

resurrection idea. Historical necessity wove the garment. The Christian conviction survived, but in a grosser form and at the expense of the pure leap of faith which is its source and origin. It survived more as a *modus operandi dei* than as a creative inspiration of the soul thirled to God. Hence the mechanical aridity of most subsequent eschatological teaching.

It is now time to turn to the question of objectivity. Many who have discarded the grosser conception of resurrection still wish to cling to what they consider to be the necessity for an objective event "of some kind."

It is not clear what is meant by objectivity in this context. An underlying assumption seems to be that what is not external to oneself is illusory. Nothing "real" can happen apart from external stimulus. This involves a psycho-physical theory which in another context would be regarded as an extreme form of behaviourism.

The most urgent psychological need for objectivity is felt to arise from the supposed impossibility of accounting for the transformation in the disciples apart from some supernatural event. But this change is itself subjective. Is it to be argued that every such change is the result of external event? Would it be argued theologically that the Holy Spirit never operates except via an objective agency of special competence, i.e. not related to the normal context of life?

Let us consider the transformation. This tends to be placed in a special category for two reasons—its dramatic intensity and its spectacular character. As regards the first, how much depends on the assumption that it took place in the space of three days at most? Yet this cannot have been the case. The whole narrative is foreshortened in the Gospels and thereby sharpened to an unnatural degree. Nothing prevents us from assuming the time necessary for a crisis of conviction to run its course.

If the vitality of the contrast between pre-Crucifixion and post-Crucifixion reactions is thus modified, it is also due to be modified still further in terms of its own content. It is generally assumed that the cause of the disciples' dejection was related to Jesus directly. But this is not so. It was related to their own psychological circumstances. Their disappointment and disillusion was with the course of events, with the part they had played, with the part of their rulers and with the fate of Jesus. But it cannot for a moment be maintained that they were disappointed in what Jesus was in Himself. Had it been otherwise no miracle could have restored faith in Him.

Once this distinction is made clear, it is clear also that what Jesus was to them, unformulated as it was, could not be annulled even by the tragedy of His fate. Nor would they have wished it to be annulled, otherwise His fate could not have become the kind of problem it was. And what He was to them they did not realise then and there but only in time, after His death—a common experience.

Unless it is felt necessary to infer that in Himself He became something quite different to them from what He had been in the days of His flesh (and how is this possible?), it is sufficient to maintain that what happened was the conscious and explicit formulation of a conviction which arose directly out of what He had always been to them. A kind of objectivity may be necessary to the expression of this experience: it is not necessary to the experience itself.

It is possible to reject the circumstantial stories in which the conviction that created the Church is incapsulated, without rejecting the conviction. But is it possible to find a halfway house between objectivity and subjectivity? Is there anything called semi-objectivity? Is there an appearance which is not physical? If there were, would not this be the same thing under a different name, felt to be necessary for the same reasons as the physical?

A crisis of conviction may be of such a nature as to require expression in objective terms in order to be communicable. It may involve what the experiencer genuinely believes to be objective factors. The point at issue, however, is whether one considers an appearance of some kind necessary as of the essence of the experience, or whether the essential in the experience is the new conviction. In the former case objectivity is imperative; in the latter it is at best contingent.

If we survey two of the most signal instances of a crisis of conviction in Scripture, that of Isaiah and that of Paul, no one thinks the experience less valid if it is regarded as personal and subjective. It is not required that we should believe that others present in the Temple at the same time as Isaiah would have seen what he saw. It is stated that Paul's companions did not.

True objectivity in these instances is therefore not regarded as essential. The question arises whether the "objectivity" which the participants reported was the agency and essence of the crisis or simply its concomitant. No one would assert that such a crisis of experience in no way depended on the concurrent life of the participant.

The Emphasis on Instruction

REFLEXION on the contents of the Gospels will show that the question dominating the minds of the Evangelists was that of the Person of Christ. It might be said that they wrote to raise and answer the question, "Who or what is Jesus?" This is the *esse* of Christian preaching, the nucleus of the cell of evangelism. It predetermines the content of Christian worship and Christian ethics. It prescribes that Christianity shall not be only a cult or a system of morality but a faith.

In Mark the question is raised in one way or another, often in the form of a direct question, by John the Baptist, the disciples, the demoniacs, the Pharisees, the official representatives of Church and state. The identity of Jesus is the basis of the Birth-narratives in Matthew and Luke. Jesus appears to be a babe in a manger, but in reality He is the King of the Jews, the Saviour of the world. This is the theme of the Fourth Gospel also, not only in the Prologue but throughout, and pointedly in the series of "I am" sayings.

That speculation on the question, "Who is Jesus?" began in His lifetime it is impossible to doubt. His words and works compelled it. In the eyes of the Evangelists they are specially important because they are evidence which leads to the answer. "Go and tell John what things ye have seen and heard" (Lk. vii.22). In all probability the question was raised first and in its simplest form in His own home town. No one is more surprised when a man surpasses expectations than the people of his own locality.

But it reached more considerable proportions as His reputation grew. He was accounted a prophet. More than a prophet? If so, how much more and what more? His fame increased. His life became the focus of rumour and speculation as He grew to the stature of a national figure in the eyes of His contemporaries. This was inevitable but there are many indications that it was not welcome.

The crisis for this speculation on the identity of Jesus, as for almost everything in the total Christian event, is the Crucifixion. From that point the question has to be asked and answered (if it is still considered important) in the light of the knowledge that He died like a criminal, if not as a criminal. The Cross is the touchstone. All that went before leads up to it; all that follows descends from it. It may be a climax of defeat and disappointment or worse; it may be a climax of vindication and glory. Which it is depends on who He is.

To the populace, to Pilate, to the Sanhedrin, the crucifixion of Jesus was the answer, final and irrevocable, that made the question no longer significant. That Jesus could be crucified was sufficient to convince the Jewish leaders that He had been an impostor. Whatever estimate Pilate made of Him, it was not high enough to forbid His being treated as a criminal. In the eyes of the people the Cross was the end, whether they regretted it or not. For all these the incident was closed. But not for some of His disciples. For them the question was still a very live issue. It had not been answered even yet and it was more urgent than ever.

We noted as one of the features of the post-Crucifixion narratives, the emphasis on instruction by the Risen Christ. On what does this instruction centre? On the necessity, the inevitability, of the Cross and the consequences that flow from it. This surely means that the interest of the disciples converges from both sides on the Crucifixion of Jesus. This is so because the Cross is the key to His identity and His identity is the question that will not let them go.

Now until this seemingly incongruous happening, the Crucifixion of Jesus, is seen as something necessary to the destiny of Jesus, there can be no answer to the question of His identity. He can remain a prophet, but if He is more than a prophet, the Cross must be more than His martyrdom; it must be seen as inseparable from His divinely ordained role—however that role is to be described.

This profound riddle was solved. The disciples had a Gospel on the other side of the Crucifixion simply because it was solved. But it was not solved and could not have been solved before the Crucifixion. The bewilderment with which the whole question of the identity of Jesus is encompassed in the Gospel records is due to a simple fact—the antedating of the solution.

After the riddle was solved, the Gospel was compounded of that solution and the Gospels, inevitably, were written in the light of it. The effect was to project the solution into the pre-Crucifixion era when, as a matter of history, the solution was not known. The story of Jesus is told by the light of an answer which could not have been known at the time of the events recorded.

Thus the story is folded back on itself so that what was known later, is supposed to have been known at a previous stage. The faith of the Evangelists makes an anachronic leap which was certain to distort the history. This antedating of the answer causes disconcerting out-cropping of the post-Crucifixion data within the pre-Crucifixion story. In the Fourth Gospel, where the Evangelist frankly begins with his conclusion, the whole story is re-phrased in the light of this conclusion. In the Synoptic Gospels also the presentation is modified but to a less degree. The intrusion of post-Crucifixion influence is therefore more obvious.

There are two fundamental matters that are raised by scholars who approach the subject of the life of Jesus from quite a different angle from our own. They are raised because of awareness of the difficulty of accepting them as and where they occur in the Gospel record. The first concerns the Messianic title and the second concerns the forecasts of the Resurrection.

Many scholars find it difficult to believe that Jesus claimed to be Messiah. The Gospels time and again represent Him as silencing any claim made by others on His behalf. At the same time it is obvious the Gospel writers fully believe that the title rightly belongs to Him. But if He was Messiah, why did He not "Tell them plainly?"

Those who take the records as they stand are bound to find this a baffling conundrum. The truth is, the question is being asked and answered when as yet it was not clearly formulated and could not have been answered at all. To the bewilderment arising from the Evangelists' understandable predisposition to write history in the light of faith, are added the sophisticated attempts of commentators to solve a historical problem by means of theological jugglery.

If the records are taken at their face value, it is impossible to escape frustrating contradictions. These arise because of the supposed necessity to claim that Jesus both was and professed to be the Messiah, and this in face of obvious indications in the records that the question had not yet presented itself in this particular form.

The usual exegesis of the difficulty is to regard as fixed the proposition that He was and claimed to be Messiah and to proceed to explain away anything to the contrary. This is done by surmising that the title in the mind of Jesus bore a completely different connotation from that which it bore in the minds of all His contemporaries, including His disciples. He was the Messiah, but not their Messiah. Thus He could not accept their use of the title and they could not know His. Hence He could neither accept nor reject the title. Only when a few of His disciples were re-educated in the true meaning of it could He welcome it.

This is surely a rather over-subtle piece of rationalisation. To accept a designation only on condition that it can be evacuated of its present content and refashioned in a different image, is anything but a plain and open proceeding; to live with such ambiguity at the core of one's being requires a kind of ambivalence which nobody associates with the mind of Jesus.

To use Messiah to convert Messiah, to cast out Satan by Satan, to conceive a new idea but dress it in a garb which makes it indistinguishable from that which it would replace, is not a programme for one whose virtue as the greatest teacher is simple direct utterance from the heart to the heart. Such a recondite scheme has no place in the pre-Crucifixion period.

If the only contemporary meaning of Messiah was so alien to the mind of Jesus as is presupposed, why use it at all? What compulsion was there? New wine should be poured into new wine-skins.

And is Jesus to be regarded as one who cared about names and titles to this extent? He who warned His hearers against saying, "Lord, Lord" was quite as likely to have warned them against saying, "Messiah, Messiah," if necessary.

Here is nothing but radical incompatibility, a tailored theory which neither haps nor hides. It is an attempt to do not only the impossible but the unnecessary. It arises because dogma has overpowered history and entered into unlawful possession.

Because the question of Jesus' identity became all-important to the Church and therefore to the Evangelists, it is imagined that this question, in the same form, was equally important to Jesus in the days of His flesh. Because the Church's and the Evangelists' answer to the question was, "Messiah, but not Jewish Messiah," it is imagined that this must have been Jesus' understanding of the matter also.

E

When we realise that the question and the answer are both antedated, the sophistries of the commentators are seen for what they are.

Incidentally, this kind of problem does not arise in the Fourth Gospel for the simple reason that this Evangelist has cut the Gordian knot. He starts with a Jesus who is *Logos*, Son, Messiah, a Jesus moreover, who in His lifetime asks a verdict on His own designation as a matter of eternal consequence. He is plainly and openly who He is; men must either acknowledge or deny: there is no dubiety.

Now this is the position of the missionary Church. But who would claim that it represents the historical situation in the pre-Crucifixion period? The Fourth Gospel solves the problem before it begins its narrative. The Synoptics are snarled up in it in the midst of their narrative. But in fact the question and answer in their urgent form were not present till after the narrative reached its conclusion. The faith of the Church about Jesus was understandably read back into the days of Jesus' ministry. But there it cannot find a congruous historical setting.

We turn now to the second matter about which scholars have been doubtful for a long time, the prophecies in the Gospels specifically referring to the Resurrection of Jesus. These are in quite a different case from either the forecasts of His death or the apocalyptic utterances regarding the end of the age. The fate of the true prophet in Israel is well defined and the execution of John the Baptist was more than a recent memory. That Jesus should be aware He was treading a path which traditionally led to rejection and death, and should say so in so many words to His disciples, is surely not to be wondered at.

Again, no prophet in the true tradition had failed to speak of the terrors and promises awaiting at the end of the age. This was one of the main reasons why he was a prophet at all. It gave point and urgency to the word of the Lord he was commissioned to utter. That Jesus was certainly a prophet, whatever more he was, and that He spoke of the imminence of the end is generally accepted, though how far this influenced His teaching is still debated.

But no prophet rose from the dead or foretold that he would.

Some scholars who reject such a prophecy on Jesus' part have argued that, if Jesus knew and foretold that He would rise from the dead, this foreknowledge would make the Crucifixion nothing more than a masque. The Cross is robbed of its profoundest quality and reduced to triviality. There is great force in this reasoning, but it is the approach of the theologian, not the historian.

The reason why the forecasts of resurrection are suspect may not be based on the limitation of Jesus' knowledge or the effects of the forecasts on the doctrine of the Person of Christ or the doctrine of Redemption. They are based simply on the impossibility of reconciling such forecasts with the main features of the story.

Mark records that on three separate occasions Jesus warned His disciples of His approaching death and consequent resurrection. There is every evidence that the disciples received and accepted the forecast of death and acted precisely as might be expected in view of it. There is no evidence that they received and accepted a forecast of resurrection, and every evidence that they did not act then or later in accordance with such an expectation.

Again, and even more clearly, the story has been folded back upon itself. It is told in the light of what the Church believed about the death and Resurrection of Jesus who was to them undoubtedly the Messiah. It is impossible to conceive that the disciples should have been told in advance of such a staggering event as the resurrection of their Master and not only should not have believed it, but should have forgotten they had ever been told. It is easier to believe they might have forgotten most of what Jesus ever said, than to credit that this unprecedented secret should have dropped out of memory without trace.

If, then, we accept these two propositions, that Jesus did not accept the Messianic title and did not forecast His bodily resurrection, this means that the disciples come to the post-Crucifixion period without any assurance about His Messiahship and without any expectation that the Cross will not have been the end of the life of Jesus. This is to say that when Jesus died they were left to wonder who He had been and why He had died. His person and His death are together one enigma.

If we now examine the teaching in the post-crucifixion narratives, these two features are prominent. Jesus spoke to them about Himself. Jesus spoke to them about the necessity of His death. These are precisely the matters on which they required enlightenment if they were to continue to stand apart from the judgment of the populace, Pilate and Caiaphas, that is to say if they were to believe and become a Church.

It is now time to notice that the one thing that could satisfy the disciples on these counts, the one thing which could at once reverse the obvious consequences of Jesus' Crucifixion and answer the question as to His identity, was the conviction that He is the Messiah, a conviction arrived at in full view of the Cross.

Here if anywhere is the birthplace of the Christian faith. We may be able to be more precise but it is certain that no Church is possible after the Crucifixion until the conviction that He who lived with the disciples, bound them to Himself by a covenant and died for them was none other than God's Messiah. This was revelation beyond all expectation and, indeed, scarcely to be adequately expressed except in terms belonging to a new age.

The additional topics of teaching mentioned in our

records are worth attention. There is first of all the future of the movement. They were instructed regarding the Kingdom of God and the plan for them as witnesses, says Luke-Acts. They were commissioned to carry the Gospel into all the world, says Matthew. They were given the Holy Spirit with a divine commission, says John.

This is the point at which they found it possible to think and plan in terms of a new and radical movement in which the aims and ideals of Jesus would go on into the future. They recognise themselves now to be the chosen associates of the Messiah through whom His work and purpose will be brought to its true fruition. This is the faith that made and sustained the Church.

The other notable factor in the narratives is the association of definite persons with the initial event. They are a small company at the beginning. Even so, our traditions are very sparing in their references to specific people. Our writers are looking down a long corridor of time. It is not very easy to detect who is there and what they are saying and doing at the very beginning. The birth of the Church is like the birth of a great man. Nobody knows what he will become and by the time he is universally recognised, everybody who ever knew him has died or forgotten, if they ever knew, what he was like as a child and what he did and said when he was a boy.

It was not to be known what the future of the Church would be, and certain that none could then have the least conception of its destiny. So much that we would like to know is forever lost. Only when those who had been present were no longer alive and able to pass on by word of mouth the story of the beginnings out of their own experience, was the need for a record fully appreciated. And then too much had sunk beyond the horizon never to come into view again.

But one figure has imprinted his memory on all the

pages that have come down to us. And the picture we have of him is clearer than that of any other. Some are mere names; others appear for a moment and then are lost forever. But Simon Peter is there at the heart of it all from the first. Why? Is it simply because he was the first to be called by Jesus at the Lake of Galilee? Is it only because he is a colourful, impetuous character?

These facts alone can scarcely account for the prominence of Peter in the records of the Church, in the Gospels, Acts and Epistles. We have singled out as one of the noteworthy features of the post-Crucifixion narratives the fact that in every account this man is in the pre-eminent place. Even the Gospel of John gives back-handed witness to this fact. We must now turn our attention to it.

The Primacy of Peter

IN our investigation into the birth of the Christian Faith, we began from the documents that bear earliest testimony to its existence. We first delimited the time and then the place. Next we examined the event itself to discover its nature.

Our conclusion so far has been that, whatever else may be said about the event which is the birth of the faith, it is inseparable from the conviction that Jesus is the Messiah, a conviction necessarily arrived at after and in spite of the Crucifixion of Jesus. This conviction is first private and then public. In its private aspect it is the birth of the faith; in its public aspect it is the birth of the Church. In traditional language these are related to the "third day" and "the Day of Pentecost" respectively.

Is it possible now to go one step further with the help of our documents and point to the first person of whom it was true to say, "He is convinced, in spite of (or even because of) the Cross, that Jesus is Messiah?" The present chapter is concerned with this possibility.

What we have to do with here is a matter of someone's personal assurance, however arrived at. Christianity has been and remains in the first instance a personal commitment. To this day nothing can be conceived as more intimate, individual and personal than a man's faith in Jesus Christ. This is true if we are thinking of Christianity in terms of the New Testament meaning of faith.

That Christianity also has its public aspect is beyond question. But hereditary Christianity which equates being a Christian with being a citizen of a Christian country or having one's name on the roll of a Christian organization, is not what the New Testament is about.   Christianity is what created the Church.   What the Church makes of Christianity may be and often has been something very different.   Christianity has begun to exist in the world when someone says, "I believe Jesus is the Messiah."   It continues for the same kind of reason.

As we have already noticed, all our documents bear witness that if anyone can be identified as the significant person it is Simon Peter.   There is no need to recount the various post-Crucifixion incidents in which he appears, but they prove beyond all doubt that in this matter Peter's role is pre-eminent.   That this is due simply to his being one of the company or to his being a colourful personality is not sufficient explanation.   He is described as being there and is revealed as a colourful personality (in the Gospels) simply because of the part he played.   He is spotlighted because he is at the centre, not because the light has been moved from the centre to spotlight him.

Now if this is a reasonable assumption, it is likely that we shall see traces of it in the Gospel narrative.   Since every other aspect of this event has cast its shadow forward into the record of the pre-Crucifixion period, it is presumable that this aspect also has done so.   The call of Peter as the first disciple may be an indication that this is so, first in time being collated with first in importance.

But immediately this question is raised, what leaps to the mind is the confession of Peter near Caesarea Philippi. An examination of this incident reveals the most pertinent relations with the total event with which we are concerned.

This has always and rightly been regarded as a key incident.   Scholars have been right in the importance they have attributed to it but wrong in not realising that its subject is exactly what it purports to be.   The result is that in attempting to find a place for it in the pre-Crucifixion ministry of Jesus (as, indeed, the documents themselves do), they have never been able to combat the violence it does to the record of the life of Jesus and the beginning of the Church.

It is the major cause of the bewilderment which we noted earlier in regard to the question of Jesus' identity and the significance of the Cross. In its present position, it misleads us on these immense issues and creates confusion in certain other directions. In its rightful place, it is supremely congruous to its own subject matter and also throws light on other matters which in its present context it only serves to obscure.

As an instance of the confusion which displacement has caused, let us consider the effect of this incident in its present place on the story of Peter's denial of Jesus.

We are required to believe that Peter's denial of any association with Jesus takes place in spite of his conviction that He is none other than the Messiah. This is utterly incomprehensible. It makes the incident a repudiation of his faith in and any association with God's anointed. This is the very act of which it is said that he who does any such thing will be disowned in the sight of God. Such an act is not simply an instance of moral cowardice: it is the only true betrayal of Messiah. It is the ultimate rejection.

But the record by itself (i.e. not read in the deflected light of the confession story) is simply an account of moral failure at the point of extreme pressure. It is a failure of nerve, not the betrayal of a sacred assurance on which a man's eternal destiny may depend.

Had it been otherwise, Peter had more reason to despair than Judas. Indeed, they must exchange places. Judas betrayed the whereabouts of Jesus but Peter denied the Messiah. If, as some think, what Judas betrayed was the Messianic secret, then he is damned for affirming that Jesus is Messiah while Peter is pardoned for denying it!

In the post-Crucifixion period the same circumstances

reveal a very different Peter. The reason is plain. He now holds a conviction about Jesus that he would rather die than surrender. Now he is sure Jesus is Messiah; before the Crucifixion he had no such certainty.

This illustration shows that the confession incident is displaced by making clear that the result of forcing it into its present position in the narrative is to make nonsense of other incidents which appear to have no direct relation to it.

We have previously noted that references to the identity of Jesus as Messiah and prophecies of resurrection are ante-dated. This incident contains both. Thus, on two different counts, the incident is palpably misplaced and obviously belongs to the period with which we are primarily concerned It is post-Crucifixion narrative.

The difficulties of commentators in treating the confession incident are eloquent in the same sense. They mostly recognise that the confession of Peter is of the utmost importance, but at the same time they are aware of the grave difficulties it raises. It is too significant to be over-looked, yet the consequences of accepting it in its present setting are confusion. The result is what might be expected and can be seen in most commentaries.

Particularly is this so with the Matthew version. Here there are additions which must be regarded by such com-mentators as later interpolations, as for instance, when Jesus is said to speak of the Church in precise terms. The usual explanation is that this is an intrusion made by the Church in order to give the prestige and authority to the Church which such a reference upon the lips of Jesus Himself could confer. The Church was founded by Christ. It is not unnatural to imagine that He should have referred to its foundations. To say that He did so is no great harm. It is true in spirit, if not in fact. Only the historian is interested in such nice distinctions.

But this will not do. The necessity for such an interpretation arises for one reason only—because the incident is misplaced. The fact that this confession incident is a true tradition which relates precisely to the subject with which it deals, the birth of the faith, and to the time at which the subject became relevant, the post-Crucifixion period.

The reference to the Church did not need to be intruded. It was the very subject of the whole incident. Not that we can take it as it stands even when it is transposed to its rightful place. But if we remove it to its true position, it is perfectly congruent with other material belonging to the same circumstances. It no longer creates confusion in regard to other apparently unrelated incidents.

It is now time to consider the confession incident itself. We see that everything in it points to the fact that here we have an event which may be second in significance only to the Cross itself. This incident points us directly to the place, the time and the person, the total object of our search. Every aspect of the incident leads straight to our goal. It is in itself in summary the story of the birth of the faith. It is far more illuminating than the story of the Transfiguration, which many are quite ready to transpose as a post-Crucifixion narrative. And it is much more obviously a post-Crucifixion narrative than the Transfiguration, although there is no difficulty in accepting the transposition of the latter.

The subjects we have been forced to find at the heart of the crucial interval are the question of the identity of Jesus, the mystery of the Cross, the birth of a conviction in which both find a common answer, namely, that Jesus is Messiah. These are the presuppositions of the faith that created the Church. Without them what we may call the incident of Jesus is at an end, as it was for everyone except the disciples and until the Church was born. Now the

Synoptic records of the Petrine confession bring together and unite them in one incident.

(It is noteworthy that the Fourth Gospel has no need of such a precise incident. It begins by assuming this union as made in Heaven. Jesus is never anything less than Messiah from the beginning; the Cross is His glorification known in advance. Andrew divines the truth from the first (1.41). Peter reiterates what they all know (VI.69). In the Fourth Gospel doubt is due to spiritual obtuseness, not to mental uncertainty. Since it is primarily theological and only incidentally historical, the Fourth Gospel provides for no evolution, no gradual unfolding and gradual realisation, only existence and the correlatives of knowledge and ignorance. But even in the Fourth Gospel Peter is inseparably associated with the confession of Messiahship. Incidentally, if we acknowledge that here the confession of Jesus as Messiah is antedated to the very beginning of the Gospel story, is there any reason to deny that it could be anachronic in the Synoptics also? The Synoptics show us history modified by theology: the Fourth Gospel shows us theology modifying history.)

The identity of the historical Jesus is a riddle, the Cross is a bewildering tragedy to His followers, and the initial discovery of the fact which unites and resolves them both takes place in the mind of one man and explains the existence of the Church.

This is precisely the subject matter of the passage we are now considering. The incident opens with the dominating question, "Who is Jesus?" The answers hitherto given are inadequate. The true, that is to say, the resolving answer is given by Peter, with the acquiescence of the other disciples. Immediately associated with this is the second crucial question which is the Crucifixion.

It is evident that this is a record of mental and spiritual conflict upon the two key themes that lie at the foundation of the Church. If He is the Christ, why the Crucifixion? If He has been crucified, can He be the Christ? This is the dilemma of the post-Crucifixion period, a dilemma which existed for those who had followed Jesus, loved Him but never understood Him, a dilemma which they could not simply abandon because their love of Him and His love of them was stronger than death.

The addition to the record of Mark which we find in Matthew's Gospel, is not an intrusion but an interpretative comment. It is proof that this staggering confession first uttered by Peter was recognised as the birth of the faith and therefore the birth of the Church. It specifically states that the Church is founded on the confession of Peter and thereby tells us that this is what was believed at the time the Gospel was written. If we ask why this was believed and for how long it had been believed, there seems no good reason to answer otherwise than that it was true and had been considered true from the start.

There are two interesting sidelights. The first is the reference to Satan and the comment which charges Peter with thinking as other men think and not as God thinks. Nothing could more plainly indicate that we are here in the presence of the kind of situation which we have in the Temptation of Jesus. The reference to Satan and to the will of God as the only valid choice enforce the parallel. This is the record of an inward conflict, presumably in the mind of Peter. What men have thought is that Jesus was a prophet but is now dead and therefore can't have been Messiah. Is Peter satisfied that this is so? The confession is the answer. Because the whole incident has been misplaced, the answer has been given before the question is stated.

The second is in the Matthew version. The blessing of Peter is consequent on his confession that Jesus is Messiah. But it is made clear that this conviction of Jesus' Messiahship did not arise in the mind of Peter because of any objective phenomenon—"Flesh and blood hath not revealed it unto thee." If this incident is transposed, then the significance of this comment is very profound and of such a character as to vindicate anew what has been said in a previous chapter regarding the accounts of post-Crucifixion appearances.

Our conclusion therefore is that the faith whose birth we have sought to trace takes its rise in the mind of Peter. He is thus truly regarded as the rock on which the Church is founded in virtue of his confession that Jesus is Messiah. This accounts for the reverence in which he was held by the Church and the prominence he enjoys in the Gospel narratives. He may not have been alone in the conviction for long, but to him goes the honour of being the first to achieve and express it and nothing can rob him of this singular privilege.

Tu es Petrus is certainly a text to conjure with. But let the conjurer beware of mistaking the nature of its power. It is a text of faith, not of dogma. Here the lamp of faith is lit but it must be set on a lampstand, not under a bushel.

A Way Ahead?

OUR argument has now come to its conclusion and must stand to be judged on its own merits as a historical critical investigation into the post-Crucifixion narratives of the New Testament.

The two main conclusions likely to be most strongly resisted are the interpretation of the Resurrection as conviction rather than event, and the transposition of the Caesarea Philippi narrative to the post-Crucifixion period. Something has been said in exposition of the former in Chapter 5. The present chapter is intended to clarify the consequences for our understanding of the Jesus of history if the latter were to be accepted.

Christianity is based not on knowledge about the life of Jesus but on belief concerning Jesus. The first preachers, we may readily accept, exhorted men to believe that Jesus is the Christ. Knowledge is bound to its data but faith is unfettered.

If, however, we persist in asking, "What do we know of Jesus?" the answer is disquieting. If our primary source for the story of Jesus is the Gospel of Mark, then from the point of view of providing the material for the history of Jesus and for an assessment of His own and His contemporaries' estimate of Himself, the Gospel has two striking deficiencies.

In the first place the material is scanty and disconnected. The story begins only when the life is nearly over and even so does not present a continuous narrative. As far as time and place are concerned we are at a loss to know, for example, how long His ministry lasted and what itinerary

He followed. Mark in itself is an unrelated series of incidents except for the Passion narrative.

But more serious is the fact that the identity of the central character is wrapped in confusion. There is no doubt as to the writer's belief that Jesus is the Messiah. But it cannot be said that it is clear how far or at what point Jesus Himself believed this and to what extent it was believed by others who knew Him. Those who make this confession in the Gospel are admonished to be silent. It is not clear that the entry into Jerusalem is of a Messianic character. No witness was found to say He regarded Himself as Messiah. His answer to the High Priest is ambiguous.

The question arises whether these facts about the nature of the document are due to a conflict between history and dogma, which was Wrede's solution, or to the character of the Messianic title, which was Schweitzer's.

Wrede was of the opinion that Mark's Gospel was written from the point of view of a belief in the Messiahship of Jesus but that such a belief had no legitimate place in the history of Jesus. This belief did not arise till after His death. It has been intruded into the story as the salient fact and is the cause of the manifest ambiguities within the Gospel.

It follows that if we are in search of history, we must discount or re-interpret those incidents in which the Messianic idea predominates. Mark's purpose was not primarily to write the life but to preach the Messiahship.

In following out this argument Wrede had to discount not only one general and prominent impression of the Gospel and some specific texts, the tenor of which was to declare or imply that the Messiahship of Jesus was known both to Jesus and to others. He had to discount the substantial story of Peter's confession at Caesarea Philippi, notably the only incident in which the Messiahship is both confessed and accepted unequivocally.

This appeared to be a disastrous proceeding since the

incident seemed to be basic to ___ ___ of the Gospel narrative. It is the climax of fait... ...in the compass of the total document. It may be said that without it there is no Gospel and therefore no possibility of a Church. To excise this incident is to leave a blank where there ought to be an answer to the most pertinent question raised by the life of Jesus as seen through the eyes of the Church.

Because this is so, Wrede was unable to substantiate his case. It was not possible to discard a key narrative which is a psychological necessity if the Gospel is to be written at all. This would be to accuse Mark not only of a dogmatic bias but of deliberate fabrication. While it can be appreciated that interpretation might modify history, this is very different from interpretation inventing history.

Schweitzer approached the problem with the idea of vindicating the Marcan hypothesis by proving that the nature of the document is due to the nature of Messiahship, not to the intrusion of dogmatic interest. His thesis was that Messiahship during the earthly life of Jesus was not actual but potential. Hence the answer to the question whether Jesus was the Christ in the days of His flesh could not be either "Yes" or "No." Jesus was the Christ and was not yet the Christ. He was *Christus futurus*. This He believed about Himself and others divined concerning Him in His lifetime. The mystery is not created by the author of Mark: it resides in the title of Messiah.

This solution has not been acceptable for the following main reasons. The first is that Schweitzer has not been able to show that the Messiah *futurus* idea is anything more than a daring guess. The distinction between "I am" and "I will be" is beyond no one's grasp. There is no mystery in it. Neither Mark nor Jesus seems to give any indication that such a distinction was the essence of what has been called the Messianic secret. The idea that such a distinction of time and tense is the key to the problem is surely academic

F

to a degree incompatible with the setting of the problem.

Secondly, as Schweitzer works out the idea he is compelled to present Jesus as in the end acting as if He were now Messiah, as if the Messianic task had to be taken up even before the Messianic age has arrived. Jesus, as Messiah-to-be, is made to force the hand of God, to attempt to bring in the Kingdom before the appointed time. This is more than is to be required even of Messiah Himself, who is to be installed only by God and in God's time, and it is not in character with the previous life and teaching of Jesus according to Mark.

Thirdly, Schweitzer showed the urgent and fanatical character of the eschatological beliefs prevalent in Jesus' day. His great service is precisely there. Never again can any account of Jesus be even attempted which fails to take note of the eschatological ethos of the period. But he did not solve the problem of Jesus' relation to eschatology.

Schweitzer made it credible that Jesus Himself entertained some of these beliefs. It is impossible to expunge them from the Gospel narrative without abandoning history and rewriting "liberal" lives of Jesus. But what lost the case in the eyes of scholars and plain unsophisticated readers of the Gospel alike, was his theory that Jesus Himself identified Himself as the personification of these beliefs. His Jesus thus became psychologically and historically incredible.

The resulting portrait, understandably, is not of the same person of whom Glover, for instance, could say, "Sense and sanity are the marks of Jesus' religion" or (to go back beyond the "liberal" tradition) the Jesus whose teaching Erasmus could describe as a "gentle philosophy." The Jesus he depicts could inspire a Jewish revolt, which the historical Jesus never did; He could not inspire a world faith, which the historical Jesus achieved.

The same kind of criticism applies to the idea that Jesus brought together in His own mind and person the Son of Man and Suffering Servant concepts. The result is equally a monstrosity.

It looks very sound to argue that he who brought these two concepts together is the founder of the Church, and that this could have been done only by Jesus. But this will not stand up.

That the two concepts were ultimately brought together is granted. But it is not a single, simple operation. Not only are the two ideas to be married, ideas that hitherto have had no apparent affinity, but someone is to say, not "He is that" but "I am that." To attribute this to Jesus is to out-Schweitzer Schweitzer. The secret of Jesus does not reside in titles and concepts but in His life.

The argument that the community (the Church) could not have united these titles and applied them to Jesus after His death is specious. This is quite a different operation psychologically and is in fact what the community did repeatedly. No one would argue that Jesus thought and spoke of Himself as the *Logos*. How then account for the Prologue of the Fourth Gospel? On the other hand, it is obvious that once Jesus is regarded as the Messiah by the Church, every other title (short of deity?) hastens to pay tribute to Him.

Now it is important to note why Schweitzer's quest ended in a cul-de-sac. It is precisely because he had not solved the problem of the relation between Jesus and the Messianic idea. It is one thing to say Jesus was a man of His age in regard to some of the beliefs he held. We may readily agree that it is a gross blunder to expect the Jesus of history to underwrite what we moderns conceive to be our noblest aspirations.

But to present Him as a man who believed He was or was about to be an apocalyptic, supra-natural being, is to identify Him with a unique form of abnormality. This puts Him beyond the range of communicable personality, a position which His life and subsequent influence make it impossible to accept.

We are not bound to have either an apocalyptic or a non-apocalyptic Jesus if by apocalyptic is meant one who believed Himself to embody apocalyptic ideals as distinct from one who held apocalyptic ideas.

This dilemma is not real. Both elements are indubitably present and neither is capable of dominating the other. We are not condemned to choose a "modern" Jesus or a Jesus so abnormal as to signify nothing except to the fanatics of His own day. And it is Wrede who points the way here to this conclusion: Jesus thought in apocalyptic terms but did not think that He Himself was Messiah.

But that road appeared to be barred. In particular the Caesarea Philippi incident was an irremovable obstruction. Attempting this road involved the idea that Jesus was not identified as Messiah till after His death. This in turn, as far as Wrede could see, meant discarding the confession at Caesarea Philippi as unhistorical—a drastic expedient.

If, however, this incident is in fact a post-Crucifixion narrative, as has been argued from quite another angle in a previous chapter, then the road is open.

The transposition of the Caesarea Philippi incident might so far have been regarded only as a new and unsupported interpretation which may or may not fit an *ad hoc* purpose, i.e. the explication of the post-Resurrection narrative. But it is now seen to be much more than this.

This interpretation of Peter's confession may do justice to the corpus of Resurrection narrative. But it will be highly significant if at the same time it suggests a new possibility in the story of our search for the Jesus of history.

The case is that the incident is rightly regarded as one which cannot be ignored or reduced in status. It is a key incident and so must remain. But in its present position it frustrates every attempt to go forward to an understanding of the Resurrection narratives or to a deeper appreciation of the life, teaching and influence of Jesus.

If, however, it is regarded as a post-Crucifixion narrative of the birth-moment of the faith, its status is certainly not diminished, it illumines the post-Crucifixion scene and it allows new hope to those who still think it worth while to seek an answer to the questions Jesus puts to mankind.

In these circumstances, it may be conceded that the issues here gathered to a focal point are of such consequence as to bespeak serious consideration for the interpretation which has been proposed.

Epilogue: Who is Jesus?

THIS is the biggest question in the world. It has evoked some of the biggest answers in the world. But those who have been satisfied with the answers have never really asked the question.

So long as description is different from essence, so long as a formula is not the same as the *res ipsa*, so long will it remain impossible to subsume under a form of words the greatest figure on the human horizon. Man, Prophet, Messiah, Son of God, God Incarnate, Second Person of the Trinity—one and all remain as pointers in the direction of the grand enigma.

The question dominates the Gospel story. It is paramount in the New Testament and in the thinking of the Christian Church throughout the centuries. It is central to every valid assessment of the destiny of the human race. To answer it requires a knowledge which is open to no one except Him in whom it resides as the reason why we ask it. Only when we can say what man is and what God is can we know the answer.

I do not expect that my reconstruction of the post-Crucifixion days will be generally acceptable. All I can hope for is that those who have persisted in asking the question at the head of this chapter will recognise it as an honest attempt. It is made out of respect for truth and reverence for Him whose life and work creates the need to seek without the hope of finding—at least in our lifetime. All who are already satisfied will regard it as mistaken if not pernicious.

Although this has not been a study of the Person of Christ, it is obvious that that is the key to the whole inquiry.

That there is a post-Crucifixion story is due to the fact that there is a pre-Crucifixion story. This is historically true, but it needs to be realised that it is theologically true as well, and that all theology which is based on the supposition of a hiatus is doomed to disappointment. To disjoin the Risen Christ from the Jesus of Nazareth is to forsake theology for theosophy, history for gnosis.

Many sincere theologically-conditioned minds will find it difficult to understand how the transpositions proposed in previous chapters can result in anything but a diminishing of the stature of Jesus. If He did not accept the title of Messiah, if He did not foretell His Resurrection, if He did not appear to His disciples in bodily form after His death, is He not therefore made inferior to what He would be had He done these things?

This is the kind of doubt which arises only when we imagine that we already know who He is and are therefore in a position to apply a measuring rod which we already possess. But clearly this is not so and cannot be so.

If He is not Messiah, is He therefore condemned to be less than Messiah? If He foretold no Resurrection, is someone who may have done so therefore superior to Him? If he did not appear as one returned from the grave, is the fact of the faith therefore more easily and less worthily explained?

We who have been brought up in the Church have mostly been given the answer before we asked the question. If the stature of Jesus is such as to account for His pre-eminence in world history, the answer we have received is at best a good pointer. It cannot be such that it obliges us to desist from the quest for a more complete answer. It cannot condemn us to regard every attempt to continue the quest as *eo ipso* a minimising of the stature of Jesus.

Nothing puts a greater stumbling-block in the path of those who wish to know who Jesus is, than the use of a creed not as a pointer but as the whole truth by which every new thought is to be judged and condemned. Believe or be damned is not a live option in the twentieth century except where authoritarianism of one kind or another has firmly set its face against the normal claims of historical research. In such circumstances we are bidden to believe and adore because we ought to, not because we are awakened to spontaneous wonder. And the danger always is that the object which authority sets before us for our good may be in large measure the creation of authority itself, with only the most tenuous relation to the world of act and fact. If tradition is to be received but never questioned in the sphere of theology only, how will this exception be justified except by a final act of resignation to the irrational?

We have never seen Christ in the flesh and never expect to see. Even those who most firmly believe in the bodily appearances are content to require them only for a limited period—Luke's traditional forty days. All Christians are blessed because they believe, even if they have not seen and never hope to see.

And what they believe is not that He once was seen on earth again after His death. This is not the content of the Christian faith; it is merely saying "Amen" to a tradition. What they believe is that He is not to be understood in terms that may be adequate for any other member of the human race, even the most illustrious. They pass from the statement that "God was with Him" to "the highest name that Heaven affords is His by sovereign right."

The faith of Peter was a conviction about a known person. The knowledge of the Person was essential to the conviction. That the conviction was accompanied by supra-historical phenomena may or may not be true. This could add nothing to the conviction and in the nature of the case must remain incommunicable as the visions and voices of Paul in the third Heaven.

The faith is the creation of Jesus mediated to the world through Peter in the first instance. Peter made the adequate answer to the question, "Who is Jesus?" By adequate I mean congruous with the need and capacity of the hour. It was not the only possible answer, nor indeed the only answer of the early Church. Nor is it the answer which is adequate today.

But when and where Christianity ceases any longer to ask the question, or is content with an answer not adequate to the hour, it has begun to fossilise—first in the individual mind and then in the life of the Church.

Christianity as an hereditary religion, a social pheno-menon, an establishment, may continue to function, but as a revelation of God and man it will have entered on its eclipse. Men will still say, "Lord, Lord," but will have ceased to understand and respond to the words and works of Jesus by which faith is born and nourished.

We believe this can never happen. Nevertheless we are in constant peril of allowing it to happen to us. When we cease to ask the question, when we are content with stock answers, when we assume that Christianity is a matter of correct creed and not a communion with Christ, when we imagine the mind can be bludgeoned into it instead of the soul drawn to it, we have left the road that all must travel who follow Jesus.

The Fourth Gospel gives us little help in the historical reconstruction of those far-off days. Its value lies in its occasional flashes of interpretive insight into the pre-dominant question. With one such we conclude our strictly limited study.

Jesus said, "I am the resurrection, and the life: he that believeth in me, though he were dead, yet shall he live: and whosoever liveth and believeth in me shall never die."

Appendix

The Position of the Caesarea Philippi Incident

QUESTIONS about order in Mark seem to have arisen almost on publication, as the famous quotation from Eusebius shows. What Papias and the Presbyter meant by "not in order" is not clear. It tends to be interpreted in the light of the interpreter's own view of the Gospel.

In recent years the text of the New Testament has been subjected to scientific analysis. Modern statistical techniques make it possible to state the characteristic features of Gospels and Epistles.

In their book *The Structure of the Fourth Gospel* (Oliver & Boyd 1961), G. H. C. Macgregor and A. Q. Morton have shown that the structure of John is quite different from that of Galatians, for instance. It may be indicated by saying that an epistle is composed, a Gospel constructed.

A. Q. Morton in *New Testament Source Analysis* (in preparation) has carried out a general examination of the six major books, i.e. the four Gospels, Acts, and Revelation. He shows there are two features of the Gospels as a whole, and of Mark in particular, which remove many of the supposed difficulties in the way of regarding the Transfiguration and Caesarea Philippi as post-Crucifixion stories.

1. The Gospels are not orderly arrangements of narratives. They are aggregations of large blocks of material. It is therefore dangerous to apply chronological tests to any single story.

Morton demonstrates that the Passion Narrative in all

Four Gospels is so uniform and consistent in sequence that all four must have a common ancestry. The whole Passion sequence must be regarded as a unit.

Papias' remark therefore cannot refer to individual stories but to these blocks. If these are not in order then the chronology is in very sketchy condition.

Mark begins with the Baptism and ends with the Passion narrative which concludes the ministry. The Transfiguration and Caesarea Philippi immediately precede the final block. They are not public but private events and their position in the Gospel says nothing as to their true chronological position.

2. The second argument from the structure of the Gospel is fully illustrated in *The Structure of the Fourth Gospel*. There Morton examines the prose of composite works. One feature is a much higher proportion of long paragraphs. He gives the rule that, of all paragraphs longer than twice the average length of paragraph in the Gospel, over 80 per cent. are discrete sources which have been copied into the book or made up from source material.

Mark has seven such paragraphs—The Gadarene Swine, the Beheading of John the Baptist, the Feeding of the Multitude, On Cleanliness, Caesarea Philippi, the Boy Epileptic, Peter's Denial. Mathematical probability indicates that four-fifths of these are copied from sources.

A narrative like Caesarea Philippi is therefore more likely than not to be copied from a source and the structure of the whole Gospel is such as to indicate that an insertion of this kind is not made in chronological order.

The author is not competent to expound what is obviously a highly technical statistical argument. What he suggests, with the concurrence of Morton who has been consulted on the point, is that the structure of Mark does not imply that the Caesarea Philippi incident is in its correct chronological order. Its present position is no handicap to an argument which aims to set it in its true position.

In conclusion, it is worth considering whether the tradition of disorder in Mark would have been handed down initially if all it referred to was misplacement of incidents within the middle section of the Gospel. It is much more certain to have been considered important if it was thought that one or more incidents included in the middle section ought to appear after the Passion Narrative.